D0572426

The Original Six Hockey Trivia Book

"The Rocket" — Maurice Richard

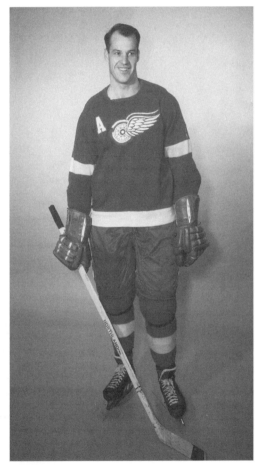

"Mr. Hockey" — Gordie Howe

Mike Leonetti

The Original Six Hockey Trivia Book

"The Big M" — Frank Mahovlich

"The Golden Jet" — Bobby Hull

Collins

The Original Six Hockey Trivia Book
© 2007 by Mike Leonetti.
All rights reserved.

Published by Collins, an imprint of
HarperCollins Publishers Ltd

No part of this book may be used or reproduced in any manner whatsoever without the prior written permission of the publisher, except in the case of brief quotations embodied in reviews.

First Edition

HarperCollins books may be purchased for educational, business, or sales promotional use through our Special Markets Department.

HarperCollins Publishers Ltd
2 Bloor Street East, 20th Floor
Toronto, Ontario, Canada
M4W 1A8

www.harpercollins.ca

Library and Archives Canada
Cataloguing in Publication

Leonetti, Mike, 1958–
The original six hockey trivia book /
Mike Leonetti. — 1st ed.

ISBN-13: 978-0-00-200763-4 ISBN-10: 0-00-200763-0

1. Hockey—Miscellanea. 2. National Hockey League—Miscellanea.
I. Title.

GV847.8.N3L466 2007 796.962 C2007-904524-3

WEB 9 8 7 6 5 4 3 2 1

Printed and bound in Canada

This book is dedicated to all those players, coaches, managers and owners — a special and select group — who have had the privilege of being associated with the "Original Six" teams.

Contents

New York Rangers   96

Toronto Maple Leafs   120

Introduction

THE ORIGINAL SIX: A LONG-LASTING LEGACY

Johnny Bower (#1) and Tim Horton (#7) of Toronto defend against Montreal's Jean Beliveau (#4).

When the National Hockey League first began play in 1917, few could have foreseen what it would bcome. In those days, it was a small, all-Canadian circuit with five members, only four of which were able to put a team on the ice — and just three completed the schedule! The league's foundations were shaky: the Montreal Wanderers dropped out after playing only four games (and defaulting two others); Toronto changed owners and nicknames after failing to complete the 1918–19 schedule (leaving just Ottawa and the Canadiens to play for the NHL championship!); Quebec moved to Hamilton a year later.

By 1924, however, the league began an impressive growth spurt. That year, a second Montreal team (the Maroons) was admitted to the league, as was the first U.S.–based entry, the Boston Bruins. Pittsburgh and the New York Americans joined the following year, and in 1926–27, three more American teams — Boston, Detroit and the New York Rangers — joined. The NHL was now a ten-team circuit, with clubs in the two most important Canadian cities as well as the most important U.S. centres.

The good times did not last, however; the Great Depression of the 1930s put a damper on the exuberance of the Roaring Twenties. The Ottawa Senators took a year off, then came back, then moved to St. Louis, where they folded after just one season. Pittsburgh moved to Philadelphia, and the Quakers were equally short-lived. The Maroons were also gone after the 1937–38 season. Wartime claimed the New York Americans (after a one-year stint as the Brooklyn Americans failed to attract fans from that borough) in 1942 and decimated powerful teams in New York and Boston.

As the 1942–43 season began, only six teams remained: the Boston Bruins, Chicago Blackhawks, Detroit Red Wings, Montreal Canadiens, New York Rangers and Toronto Maple Leafs. This lineup remained consistent for 25 seasons, coming to be known as the "Original Six."

The period between 1942 and 1967 was the golden era of hockey for fans who witnessed the sport when it was, simply, at its best. Games were played with a hard-nosed intensity — fewer than 120 steady jobs existed in the NHL, which meant that players (nearly all of them born in Canada) were the best of the best in terms of skill and talent. Still, they needed to compete fiercely to keep their scarce jobs, since there were hundreds of eager (and in many cases quite capable) minor-leaguers and top junior stars looking to crack a lineup. It was a prosperous time to be the owner of an NHL team, as the postwar boom meant that arenas were consistently packed. Games began to be televised in the early 1950s, making such stars as Maurice Richard, Gordie Howe, Bobby Hull, Frank Mahovlich, Andy Bathgate and Johnny Bucyk that much more recognizable (especially so because only a very few wore helmets or face masks).

In 1967, the NHL doubled in size overnight, adding teams in Pittsburgh, St. Louis, Philadelphia (all of whom had been in the league previously), Minnesota, Los Angeles and Oakland. Further expansion took place in 1970, '72 and '74, boosting membership to 18 teams — plus another 14 in the upstart World Hockey Association. The level of play started to drop — slowly at first, and then more noticeably. Stick-handling became a lost art as teams de-emphasized puck possession and switched to a dump-and-chase style. Less skilled players started to clutch and grab, and fighting became too prevalent.

Further expansion took place throughout the 1990s, with the result that the NHL is now a 30-team league with franchises in such unlikely locales as Nashville, Columbus, Carolina and Tampa Bay. Longtime fans have had to endure a great deal of pain as the league left traditional centres like Winnipeg, Quebec and New England for places where the game is still developing a following and is underappreciated. And with more than 700 players skating in the NHL each year, it's easy to understand if even the most ardent hockey fans have trouble knowing all of them.

However, these developments have never dimmed the lustre of the teams that make up the "Original Six." Put on a sweater of one of those teams and you will always be remembered. The logos of Montreal, Toronto, Boston, Chicago, Detroit and New York are still very distinctive and instantly identifiable. There may no longer be as many Canadian-born players on these teams, but even the U.S.– and European-born players realize that being on the roster of one of these six squads is very special. The Canadiens (23), Leafs (11, plus one each as the Arenas and St. Patricks) and Detroit (10) are still the most frequent Stanley Cup champions; among expansion teams, only the Edmonton Oilers (five), New York Islanders (four) and New Jersey Devils (three) have won as many titles as the Bruins (five), Rangers (four) and Blackhawks (three). While the Canadiens and Bruins no longer dominate the league as they did in the 1970s, and the Stanley Cup droughts endured by the Blackhawks and Leafs are now measured in decades rather than years, the Red Wings have managed to regain their position of prominence.

This is important because the NHL's popularity was at its peak in the early 1990s, when the Canadiens (1993) and Rangers (1994) claimed the Stanley Cup, the Blackhawks reached the finals (1992) and the Leafs came within a Wayne Gretzky high stick of meeting the Habs in the 1993 finals. Consider the 1992–93 campaign, when Boston had 109 points; Chicago, 106; Detroit, 103; Montreal 102 and Toronto had 99. Much of the excitement in both seasons was due to the fact that all the "Original Six" teams had a chance to win the championship. The NHL can only hope that the six squads once again find themselves in contention at the same time.

This trivia book pays tribute to the six teams that helped make the NHL what it is today. Without the solid foundation provided by these clubs, there is no way the league would have grown into a 30-team entity. The entire history of each team is covered, with 140 questions and answers per team. In addition, many photos have been selected to help evoke some of the great games, award winners, memorable trades, notable players from the past and other interesting points that make up the legacy of these six special teams. Many of today's hockey fans have had little exposure to the glory days of the "Original Six," so this book will help provide them with a sense of the history of each of these franchises. But the present day is not overlooked: many questions (and some photos) focus on events from the past three years.

Any reader of this book, young or old, will learn why broadcasters, writers and hockey analysts in general always get excited about a game that features an "Original Six" matchup. There's nothing else like it in hockey!

BOSTON BRUINS

Phil Esposito was acquired by the Boston Bruins in a major trade in May of 1967.

MEMORABLE GAMES

1) In their first NHL season, 1924–25, the Boston Bruins failed to make the playoffs, winning 6 games while losing 24. They did win their first-ever NHL contest played at the Boston Arena. Who did the Bruins beat, and what was the final score?

2) On November 20, 1928, the fabled Boston Garden opened for a game between the Bruins and the Montreal Canadiens. What was the result of the contest?

3) The Bruins won their first-ever Stanley Cup on March 29, 1929, winning the final game of the best-of-three series 2–1 over the New York

Bruin captain Milt Schmidt makes a presentation to Maple Leaf netminder Turk Broda.

Rangers. Who scored the Cup-winning goal for Boston?

4) During the 1929–30 season the Bruins won 38 games while losing only 5 and tying one. The Boston club made it to the Stanley Cup finals, but something that had not happened all year long derailed the Bruins' hopes on April 3, 1930, in Montreal. What was it?

5) After many years of losing in the playoffs, the Bruins finally climbed back to the top of the mountain by winning the Stanley Cup in 1939. Boston defeated Toronto 3–1 on April 16 to win their second championship. Who scored the Cup-clinching goal?

6) A January 18, 1941, contest saw the Bruins beat the Maple Leafs 1–0 on home ice. The goal was a special milestone for one Bruin player. Who was the player, and what was the milestone?

7) On April 12, 1941, the Bruins defeated the Detroit Red Wings 3–1 to clinch the Stanley Cup for the third time in their history. The Boston victory marked the four-game sweep of a best-of-seven final. Who scored the winning goal to cap this memorable series for the Bruins?

8) A November 27, 1941, contest between Boston and the Brooklyn Americans went into overtime with the score tied 2–2. At the time, overtime consisted of a 10-minute period that was played to its conclusion, no matter who scored — or how often. How did the Bruins fare in this contest?

9) Longtime Bruin star Bobby Bauer came out of retirement on March 18, 1952, to play one

game with former linemates Milt Schmidt and Woody Dumart. It was Bauer's only game of the season, and he scored a goal and added an assist, but it was another player who scored his 200th career goal on the same night. Name him.

10) What did Boston netminder "Sugar" Jim Henry achieve in three consecutive home games on March 7, 11 and 14, 1954?

11) The night of January 18, 1958, was a historic night for the NHL and the Bruins because the first black man played for Boston in the contest against the Montreal Canadiens. Can you name the player who broke the NHL's colour barrier?

12) Boston beat Detroit in five games during the 1957 semi-finals to gain a spot in the Stanley Cup finals against the Montreal Canadiens. The Habs took the Cup in five games, but not before the Bruins took one contest 3–0 on home ice on April 14. Which Bruin netminder recorded the shutout?

13) The Bruins were back in the Stanley Cup finals in 1958, but they lost once again to the Canadiens, this time in six games. In the semi-finals, the Bruins knocked off the New York Rangers in six games. A key game in that series was the second contest, played on March 27, in which the Bruins scored in overtime to win 4–3. Which Bruin scored the winning goal?

14) Perhaps the most memorable game in Bruins history was played on May 10, 1970, when Bobby Orr scored in overtime to give Boston the Stanley Cup for the first time since 1941. Boston beat St. Louis 4–3 to capture the Cup after just 40 seconds of extra time. Which player passed the puck to Orr to set up the winner?

15) The 1970–71 season saw the Bruins shatter just about every offensive NHL record on route to a 57-win season. However, they were shocked in the first round of the playoffs when Montreal knocked them out in seven games. The final game of the series was played in Boston on April 18, with Montreal winning the contest 4–2 due to the stellar netminding of a goalie the Bruins once owned. Name him.

16) May 11, 1972, saw the Bruins clinch their fifth Stanley Cup with a 3–0 victory on Madison Square Garden ice in the sixth game of the final. Bobby Orr scored the winner against New York in the first period, while another Bruin scored

Boston netminder "Sugar" Jim Henry tries to sweep the puck away from Toronto forward Harry Watson.

twice in the third to finish off the Rangers. Who scored the last two Boston goals?

17) The 1974 playoffs saw the Bruins romp past Toronto (in four games) and Chicago (in six) to reach the Stanley Cup finals against Philadelphia. The Bruins won the first game 3–2 in Boston on a late goal by Bobby Orr, and they nearly had the second game locked up, but a Flyer goal late in regulation time evened the score at 2–2. Who scored the game-winner for the Flyers to even the series?

Don Simmons played goal for the Bruins for five seasons before he was dealt to the Maple Leafs.

18) The Bruins were back in the Stanley Cup finals in 1977 after knocking off Los Angeles and Philadelphia in the first two rounds of the post-season. The Bruins got past the Flyers easily in four straight games. They won each of the first two games of the series in overtime. Which Bruin scored after 2:57 of extra on April 24, and which Bruin scored after 30:07 of overtime on April 26?

19) Boston made life difficult for the Montreal Canadiens during the 1978 Stanley Cup finals before losing to the mighty Habs in six games. The highlight for the Bruins came in the fourth game, when they got an overtime goal to beat Montreal 4–3 to even the series at two games each. Who scored the overtime winner for the Bruins at home on May 21, 1978?

20) The Boston Bruins held Phil Esposito Night on December 3, 1987, and as part of the festivities his sweater number was retired and a banner raised to the roof of Boston Garden. Ray Bourque, who was wearing number 7 for the Bruins, surprised Espo and everyone else watching by doing what?

21) Even though the Bruins made it to the Stanley Cup finals in 1988, there was little for Boston fans to cheer about as the Edmonton Oilers won the series handily. Something very unusual happened at Boston Garden on the night of May 24 as the Oilers tried to sweep the Bruins. What happened that caused the game to be halted with the score tied 3–3?

22) The first game of the 1990 Stanley Cup finals featured an epic battle between the Bruins and the Edmonton Oilers. The game was tied 2–2 and went to a second overtime period before it was settled at 15:30 of the second extra session. The Bruins missed many chances

to score, but a little-used Oiler scored the winner. Name him.

23) The goaltender for the Quebec Nordiques had a very busy evening when his team played the Bruins in Boston on the night of March 21, 1991. He faced 73 Boston shots, yet still managed to help his team escape with a 3–3 tie. Can you name the Quebec goalie?

24) When the Boston Bruins opened their new arena (now known as the TD Banknorth Garden) on October 7, 1995, they played to a 4–4 tie with the New York Islanders. The first goal in the new building was scored by a Bruin, while another Boston player recorded a hat trick. Can you name both players?

Joe Thornton was captain of the Bruins between 2002 and 2005.

A native of Copper Cliff, Ontario, Jerry Toppazzini scored 148 career goals with the Bruins.

25) The NHL All-Star Game was played in Boston on January 20, 1996, and it featured a game-winning goal by a Bruin to give the Eastern Conference a 5–4 edge over the Western Conference. Which Bruin scored the goal in the final minute of play?

26) He became the first Bruin since Adam Oates in 1994 to record 100 points in a season. He hit the century mark on April 4, 2003, during an 8–5 home-ice win over Buffalo. He finished the 2002–03 season with 101 points. Name the high-scoring Bruin.

27) This outstanding defenceman played most of his career with the New York Rangers but was dealt to the Maple Leafs in 2004. He was signed as a free agent by the Bruins for the 2005–06 season and he recorded 32 points (5 goals, 27 assists) — including his 1,000th career point, in a 4–3 loss to Montreal on October 18, 2005. Who is he?

28) This outstanding rookie had 106 points in 81 games during the 2005–06 season. His 100th point of the year came against the Bruins when they dropped a 2–1 decision on April 10, 2006. Who is he?

RECORDS AND AWARDS

1) Nicknamed "The Edmonton Express," this Bruin defenceman won the Hart Trophy as the NHL's most valuable player for the first time in 1933. He won it again in 1935, 1936 and 1938. Name him.

2) The Bruins claimed the rights to this centre when the players of the defunct St. Louis Eagles were dispersed in a draft held on October 15, 1935, and he went on to win the Hart Trophy twice (1941 and 1943) and record 536 points in 508 games as a Bruin. Can you name him?

3) The 1939–40 season saw three Boston players lead the NHL in scoring. Can you list them in order and recall what else they had in common?

4) Although the Bruins missed the playoffs during the 1943–44 season (finishing in fifth place with a 19–26–5 record), they did have the NHL's leading point producer on their team, with 82 points (36G, 46A) in 48 games. Can you name him?

5) This Hall of Fame netminder won the Vezina Trophy a total of four times (1930, 1933, 1936 and 1938) while he was a member of the Boston Bruins. He also backstopped the Bruins to their first Stanley Cup title in 1929. His given name was Cecil, but he was much better known by his nickname. Who was he?

6) Known as "Mr. Zero," this Bruin netminder lead his team to two Stanley Cups (1939 and 1941) and was named an NHL All-Star on eight occasions (twice on the first team, six times on

Derek Sanderson (#16) was the rookie of the year in the NHL in 1968.

the second team). The two-time Vezina Trophy winner finished his Hall of Fame career with one season in Chicago. Name him.

7) On March 4, 1941, the Boston Bruins set an NHL record by taking 83 shots on goal against the Chicago Blackhawks. The Bruins managed to score only three goals, winning the contest 3–2. Who was the netminder who stopped 80 Bruin shots?

Boston goaltender Jack Gelineau stops Toronto's Sid Smith in close.

8) The first time a Bruin won the Calder Trophy as the NHL's best rookie was in 1950, when a Boston netminder posted a 22–30–15 record with three shutouts in 67 games. He would play another full season with Boston before being traded to Chicago. Can you name this goalie?

9) Boston claimed this small right winger from the Quebec Aces of the Quebec Hockey League in 1956 and saw him win the Calder Trophy in 1956–57 after a 14-goal season. He scored 11 goals the next year, but was claimed on waivers by Toronto in January 1959. He scored a total of 41 goals in his 280-game NHL career. He later became the general manager of the Los Angeles Kings. Name him.

10) The 1963–64 season saw this Boston goaltender play every minute of all 70 games the last-place Bruins played that year. It was the last time a goalie played every minute for his team in an

NHL regular season. Who was this durable and brave goaltender?

11) After Bobby Orr broke into the NHL for the 1966–67 season, he was awarded the Calder Trophy with 41 points (including 13 goals) in 61 games played. The runner-up for the award was another defenceman, who played for Chicago. He also appeared in 61 games that season, but only had 19 points. Can you name him?

12) True or false: Bobby Orr won four major individual NHL trophies in 1970.

13) He was the first player to record his 1,000th career point as a Bruin, and he also holds the team record for most points (116) in one season by a left winger. Name him.

14) Only two players, Johnny Bucyk and Phil Esposito, have scored their 500th career goals

as members of the Boston Bruins. Which goalies allowed the milestone markers?

15) Acquired in a trade with the New York Rangers, this centre recorded his 1,000th career point on April 3, 1977, during a 7–4 Boston win over Toronto. Who was he?

Larry Regan (middle of photo) was a Bruin for two seasons before the Maple Leafs claimed him on waivers in 1959.

16) Since 1982, the NHL has awarded the William M. Jennings Trophy to the goaltender(s) whose team allows the fewest goals during the regular season. The Bruins have only won this award once, in 1989–90. Two goalies shared the honour; one of them was Andy Moog. Who was the other?

17) This centre holds the Bruins' team record for goals in one season by a rookie, with 44 in 1981–82. Name him.

18) This centre holds the Bruins' team record for points in one season, with 102 (32 goals and 70 assists) in 1992–93. Who was he?

19) The Bruins' team record for most points by a player in one game is seven, first set by Bobby Orr, who had three goals and four assists against the New York Rangers on November 15, 1973. Since that time, three other Bruins have equalled the feat. Can you name them?

20) This perennial All-Star defenceman holds the NHL record for most career points (1,579) by a blueliner. He recorded his 1,000th career

point when the Bruins tied Washington 5–5 on February 29, 1992. Name him.

21) How many different Boston Bruin players have scored 50 or more goals in one season?
a) 3 b) 4 c) 5

22) This enforcer was known primarily for his days as a Montreal Canadien, but he was with the Boston Bruins on March 31, 1991, when he set an NHL record by recording 10 penalties in one game (during a 7–3 win versus the Hartford Whalers). Can you name him?

23) This Bruin rookie recorded three assists in his first game with the team when Boston tied the Ottawa Senators 4–4 on December 5, 2000. Can you name him?

24) Since the start of the new century, only two Bruin players have been selected as end-of-the-season NHL All-Stars. Both made the second team. Can you name them?

25) Even though he was just in his second full year with the Bruins, this Quebec-born youngster

led the team in scoring during the 2005–06 season with 73 points in 81 games. Name him.

26) This large defenceman (six foot nine, 260 pounds) was named to the NHL's All-Rookie team in 1998, was a first-team All-Star in 2004 and a second-team All-Star in 2006. He signed with the Bruins as a free agent on July 1, 2006. Who is he?

27) Originally drafted by the New York Rangers (97th overall in 1995), this centre also played with the Calgary Flames and Atlanta Thrashers (where he had a 97-point season in

Goaltender Eddie Johnston played with the Bruins between 1962 and 1973.

2005–06) before joining the Bruins as a free agent and leading the team in points in 2006–07. Who is he?

28) Although he had a more-than-respectable rookie season with the Bruins in 2005–06 (69 points in 82 games) and recorded the only Bruin hat trick of the season (against Carolina on March 18, 2006), Brad Boyes quickly fell out of favour and was dealt to the St. Louis Blues in 2006–07. Who did the Bruins get in return?

TRADES

1) Ralph "Cooney" Weiland, a two-time Stanley Cup winner as a Bruin (1929 and 1939), began his NHL career with Boston and played with them between 1928 and 1932. He was sold to the Ottawa Senators in 1932, but was re-acquired in 1935 through a trade with Detroit. Who did the Bruins send to the Red Wings to complete the deal?

2) Charlie Sands was a member of the Bruins' Stanley Cup–winning team in 1939, but he was dealt away to Montreal along with Ray Getliffe on October 10 of that year. Who did the Bruins receive in return?

3) When Boston acquired goalie Terry Sawchuk from Detroit in 1955, they hoped that their goaltending problems had been solved for years to come. It didn't turn out that way, and the Bruins did Sawchuk a favour by dealing him back to the Red Wings on July 24, 1957, in exchange for which player?

4) Don McKenney, the Lady Byng Trophy winner in 1960, played in 529 games as a Bruin between

Zdeno Chara had 43 points for the Bruins in 2006–2007.

1954 and 1963, scoring 195 goals and 462 points. On February 4, 1963, he was traded to the New York Rangers, along with Dick Meissner. Who did the Bruins receive in return?

5) One of the most versatile players ever to play in the NHL, Doug Mohns began his career with the Bruins in 1953–54 and played in 710 games for Boston (recording 347 points). Mohns was traded away to the Chicago Blackhawks on June 8, 1964. Boston received two players in return. Name both of them.

6) After playing in 101 games for the Boston Bruins and recording 178 penalty minutes, tough-guy left winger Reggie Fleming was on the move again on January 10, 1966, this time to the New York Rangers. Who did the Rangers send back to Boston?

7) Defenceman Gary Doak was acquired by the Bruins in a trade with the Detroit Red Wings on February 18, 1966, and was on the Stanley Cup team of 1970. He would go on to play in 609 games with Boston (during two different stints) before leaving the team in 1981. Can you name the Hall of Fame defenceman the Bruins sent to Detroit to complete the deal in '66, as well as all the other players involved?

Bobby Orr's first season in the NHL was 1966–67, the last year of the "Original Six."

8) The greatest trade in the history of the Boston Bruins took place on May 15, 1967, when the Bruins acquired Phil Esposito from the Chicago Blackhawks. Can you name all the players involved in the trade?

9) The Bruins acquired Mike Walton as part of a three-way deal involving Toronto and Philadelphia on February 1, 1971. Can you name the two players Boston sent to the Flyers to complete their part of the deal?

Johnny Bucyk (#9) tries to score on Maple Leaf netminder Johnny Bower.

10) The Bruins wanted to bolster their defence during the 1971–72 season, and they focused their efforts on acquiring Carol Vadnais of the California Seals. The deal cost the Bruins three players, while the Seals threw one other player into the transaction. Name all the other players involved in the deal.

11) A member of two Stanley Cup teams (1970 and 1972) who registered 409 points in 448 games with the Bruins, centre Fred Stanfield was dealt away to the Minnesota North Stars on May 23, 1973. Who was the goaltender Boston got in return?

12) The Bruins made a nice pickup when they acquired right winger Bobby Schmautz from the Vancouver Canucks on February 7, 1974. He would score 135 goals and 295 points in 354 games for the Bruins. Which two players did the Bruins send to Vancouver to complete the deal?

13) Right winger Rick Middleton scored 402 goals in 811 games as a Boston Bruin after he was acquired in a deal with the New York Rangers on May 26, 1976. Who did the Bruins send to the Rangers?

14) When Buffalo signed Bruin free agent Andre Savard on June 11, 1976, the Boston club was compensated for the loss with a centre who would score 263 goals in 595 games as a Bruin. Who was he?

15) The Bruins were able to select Ray Bourque eighth overall in the 1979 Entry Draft by making a deal with the Los Angeles Kings on October 8, 1978. Name the goaltender the Bruins sent to Los Angeles in exchange for the pick.

16) Everyone hoped goaltender Jim Craig, a member of the 1980 U.S. Olympic gold medal–winning team, would revive his NHL career when the Bruins acquired him from Atlanta on June 2, 1980. He would play in only 33 games with Boston. What did Boston give up to get the ineffective Craig?

Boston defenceman Leo Boivin (#20) was one of the hardest-hitting players in NHL history.

17) The Bruins made a very good selection when they took Brad McCrimmon 15th overall in the 1979 Entry Draft. On June 9, 1982, they traded him away to Philadelphia. Name the goalie the Flyers sent to Boston.

18) On October 24, 1985, the Bruins acquired left winger Charlie Simmer from the Los Angeles Kings. The two-time 50-goal scorer had three very good years in Boston and won the Masterton Trophy in 1986. Who did the Bruins send to the Kings to complete the deal?

19) Boston general manager Harry Sinden stole future Hall of Famer Cam Neely from the Vancouver Canucks when he swung a trade for the rugged right winger on June 6, 1986. Who did the Bruins give up in the deal, and what else did they get back in return?

20) Goaltender Andy Moog, who had won a Stanley Cup with the Edmonton Oilers,

wanted to be a number one goalie and get out from under the shadow of Grant Fuhr in Edmonton. The Bruins paid dearly to acquire him. Who did they send to Edmonton to complete the deal on March 8, 1988?

21) The Bruins selected Steve Kasper with their third choice in the 1980 Entry Draft, and the checking centre went on to record 355 points in 564 games as a Bruin. He was dealt to Los Angeles on January 23, 1989, in exchange for a player once deemed to be a future superstar. Who did the Bruins receive in the deal?

22) When the Hartford Whalers signed defenceman Glen Wesley in August of 1994, the Bruins were compensated with three first-round draft choices (in 1995, 1996 and 1997). Who did the Bruins select with the choices?

23) Although the trade the Bruins made to acquire youngsters Jason Allison and Anson Carter cost the Bruins three veteran players, it was still a good deal for Boston. Which three players were sent to Washington on March 1, 1997, to complete the transaction?

24) When the Bruins decided to trade defenceman Kyle McLaren, there were plenty of teams interested in the six-foot four-inch 225-pounder. The San Jose Sharks made the deal with the Bruins, sending two players in return on January 23, 2003. Can you name both of them?

25) Boston drafted defenceman Shaone Morrisonn 19th overall in 2001, but after only 41 games with the Bruins he was dealt to the Washington Capitals with two draft choices on March 3, 2004. Who did the Bruins receive in return?

26) It had to be one of the worst deals in Bruins history — one that ultimately cost Boston general manager Mike O'Connell his job — when top centre Joe Thornton was dealt to San Jose during the 2005–06 season. Which players did the Bruins get back from the Sharks?

27) Defenceman Nick Boynton was selected 21st overall by Boston in 1999, and he went on to play 299 games with the Bruins, recording 84 points (22 goals, 62 assists) to go along with 397 penalty minutes. He was dealt to Phoenix prior to the start of the 2006–07 season. Who did the Bruins receive in return?

28) When the Bruins realized they could not sign defenceman Brad Stuart to a new contract, he

Goaltender Pete Peeters posted a 91–57–16 career mark with Boston.

was dealt to Calgary along with Wayne Primeau. Which two players did Boston get back in the February 2007 transaction?

REMEMBER HIM?

1) On October 25, 1928, the Boston Bruins sent cash to the Ottawa Senators to acquire a left winger who had won the Stanley Cup four times with the Canadian-based club. He was named coach of the Bruins and also played in 23 games for the Cup-winning Boston squad. He was elected to the Hall of Fame as well. Can you name him?

A hard-nosed right winger with a good scoring touch, Ken Hodge (#8) was a Bruin from 1967 to 1976.

2) These two brothers were both born, seven years apart, in England, and went on to play for the Bruins. The older sibling joined the Boston club in 1928–29, but a trade to Toronto kept him from celebrating the Bruins' Stanley Cup win that season. The younger brother won three Stanley Cups (one with the Rangers and two with the Red Wings) before he joined the Bruins in 1937–38. He would win the Cup with Boston in 1939, recording 25 points in 48 games during the regular season. Can you name these two brothers?

3) The Bruins sent one the best defencemen in NHL history, William "Flash" Hollett, to the Detroit Red Wings in 1944 for one of the toughest blueliners in the league. The player the Bruins picked up in the trade had led the NHL in penalty minutes while he was with the Brooklyn Americans in 1941–42, and he accomplished the same feat with Boston in 1944–45. He recorded more than 20 points four times with the Bruins before he was dealt to the New York Rangers in 1949. Name him.

4) On August 16, 1949, the Bruins swung a five-player trade with Detroit in which they gave up Pete Babando, Clare Martin, Lloyd Durham and Jimmy Peters in return for Pete Horeck and a future Hall of Fame defenceman who would play seven seasons with the Bruins. The blueliner was selected to the first All-Star team in 1951 and the second All-Star team in 1953 while with Boston. His brother also played one season with the Bruins in 1950–51. Can you name him?

5) This centre started his career with the New York Rangers in 1955–56, but the Bruins claimed him from the Montreal Canadiens in the Intra-League Draft of 1957. He scored 30 goals for the Bruins in 1957–58, but his best season came in 1959–60, when he tied Bobby Hull of Chicago for the most goals (39) and, with 80 points, fell just one short of Hull for the league lead in that category. He would also play for Chicago, Toronto and Minnesota before retiring. Name him.

6) Nicknamed "The Haileybury Comet," this tough right winger played with the Bruins from 1951–52 to 1960–61, scoring 16 or more

Centre Adam Oates (#12) was a noted playmaker throughout his NHL career.

goals five times. His best total was 24 goals in 1954–55. He was traded to Detroit in a 1961 deal that brought Murray Oliver to Boston. Can you name him?

Bruin defenceman Bill Quackenbush tries to help goalie Jim Henry against a Maple Leaf scoring effort.

7) In just his second season in the NHL, this right winger scored 19 goals for the Bruins in 1952–53. Two years later, he scored 18, but Boston sent him to Detroit in a trade in June 1955. After just 38 games as a Red Wing, the native of Timmins, Ontario, was traded back to Boston and he scored 11 times in 25 games to close out the season. He scored a career-best 31 times in 1956–57 and earned a spot on the NHL's second All-Star team, but his career was over only two years later. Who was he?

8) He played eight seasons with the Bruins from 1947–48 to 1954–55 and was named to the NHL's second All-Star team on one occasion, in 1953–54, when he scored 16 goals and totalled 47 points in 70 games. He was dealt to Detroit in 1955 and finished his career with Chicago that same year. Name him.

9) A native of Detroit, Michigan, this centre was acquired by the Bruins in the Intra-League Draft of 1959. He played with Boston for four full seasons and had his best year in 1960–61, when he scored 15 goals and totalled 41 points in 70 games. He was one of the first NHL players to wear a helmet (to protect an injury) and was named player-coach of the Minnesota North Stars during the 1969–70 season. Name him.

10) This hard-nosed left winger won three Stanley Cups with the Detroit Red Wings before the Bruins acquired him in a trade. He had four straight years of 20 or more goals with Boston (scoring a career-high 29 in 1959–60) and helped the Bruins get to the finals twice (in 1957 and 1958). He was dealt back to Detroit in 1961 and played his last two and half years with the Red Wings. He also went on to coach Philadelphia, California and Vancouver. Who was he?

11) This rugged Hall of Fame defenceman began his 910-game NHL career with Boston in 1944–45 but was dealt to Toronto in 1950 (where he won his only Stanley Cup, in 1951). The Bruins jumped at the chance to re-acquire him in 1954, and he led the league in penalty minutes during the 1954–55 season with 150. The Bruins named him team captain in 1955 and he played until the 1960–61 season. Name him.

12) A member of the U.S. Olympic gold medal–winning team in 1960, this native of Duluth, Minnesota, first joined the Bruins for 26 games during the 1961–62 season. His first

Right winger Leo Labine scored 123 career goals as a Bruin between 1951–52 and 1960–61.

full season in the NHL saw him score a career-high 23 goals, but the right winger would never score more than 18 while in Boston. He was traded to Minnesota in 1969 and would also suit up for California and Washington (he scored 22 for the Capitals in 1974–75) before his career was over. Can you name him?

13) As a rookie with the Bruins in 1963–64, this big (six foot one and 190 pounds) right winger recorded 22 points (12 goals, 10 assists), but then recorded only two points during the next 30 games he played with Boston over the next two seasons. The Philadelphia Flyers claimed him in the Expansion Draft of 1967 and he

stayed there the rest of his career, winning two Stanley Cups (in 1974 and 1975). He went on to be a television colour analyst. Who is he?

14) This French-Canadian left winger had two tours of duty with the Boston Bruins and he recorded a season of more than 20 goals on both occasions. Boston first acquired him from New York in the Intra-League Draft of 1958, and he scored 24 times in 1959–60. He was dealt to Montreal during the 1960–61 season, but the Bruins took him back in the Intra-League Draft of 1962 and he promptly scored 21 goals for Boston in 1962–63. The Philadelphia Flyers took him in the Expansion Draft of 1967 and he played the rest of his NHL career there, finishing with 383 points in 863 games. Who was he?

15) Boston picked up this tough defenceman from the Montreal organization in 1960 and he would go on to play in 620 games as a Bruin and record 1,029 career penalty minutes. He was there for all of the lean years of the 1960s, but was still in Beantown when the team improved. A nomination to the NHL's second All-Star team in 1969 was a just reward, but a stick-swinging incident nearly cost him his NHL career. Despite a serious head injury, he was able to return to play on the Bruins' Stanley Cup team of 1972. Who was he?

16) One of the best two-way players ever to suit up for the Bruins, this left winger played his entire 868-game NHL career with Boston. He played his first game for the team in 1965–66 and would score 20 or more goals seven times in his career. He was a member of the Stanley Cup–winning teams of 1970 and 1972. Known as one of the best checking wingers in hockey,

he finished second to Bob Gainey in 1979 for the Frank Selke Trophy, which recognizes the top defensive forward in the NHL. Can you name this valuable Bruin?

17) A native of Waterloo, Ontario, this centre/winger played with the Bruins during the 1969–70 season and scored seven goals and totalled 23 points in 68 games. He added one goal in 11 playoff games when the Bruins won the Stanley Cup, but was then traded to the St. Louis Blues before the next season began. The Bruins got a first-round pick in return. He would also play for New York Rangers and the Buffalo Sabres. Who was he, and who did the Bruins take with the first-round selection?

18) A career minor-league goalie, this native of Toronto, Ontario, played in three seasons for the Bruins and posted a remarkable record for an unknown. From 1972–73 to 1974–75 he appeared in 54 games and posted a mark of 37 wins, seven losses and six ties during the regular season. In spite of this terrific performance he never appeared in the NHL again after the 1974–75 season. Who was this goalie?

19) A native of North Battleford, Saskatchewan, this small but sturdy centre began his NHL career with the Bruins in 1972–73 by scoring 24 goals in 69 games. He would go on to post three seasons of 30 or more goals with the Bruins and would play in two

Stanley Cup finals (1974 and 1978) with the club. He was traded to Atlanta for defenceman Dick Redmond in 1978. Who was he?

20) This defenceman was signed as a free agent by Boston in 1974 and would play his entire 754-game career with the Bruins before going on to coach the team. The native of Brighton, Massachusetts, was a rugged blueliner (he recorded over 100 penalty minutes nine times in his career) and displayed a feisty nature both on and off the ice. He scored 49 career goals and totalled 238 points as a Bruin between 1975 and 1987. He coached the Bruins to one Stanley Cup finals appearance in 1991. Name him.

21) Known as one of the toughest players in the NHL when he played for the Bruins from 1976 to 1980, this left winger was signed as a free agent after playing three games for the St. Louis Blues in 1973–74. His best year in Boston saw him score 28 goals and 46 points in 1978–79, and he racked up more than 100

Boston left winger Real Chevrefils takes a shot on Toronto netminder Harry Lumley. Chevrefils scored 101 career goals as a Bruin.

minutes in penalties in three seasons. However, he soon fell out of favour with management and was lost in the Waiver Draft to the Quebec Nordiques. He also played for the Colorado Rockies and the New Jersey Devils. Who was he?

Hall of Fame defenceman Fern Flaman (middle of photo) moves in to help goaltender Don Simmons.

22) This centre was picked up on waivers by the Bruins in January 1985 after he had had a long career with the Los Angeles Kings and won four Stanley Cups with the New York Islanders. He recorded 13 goals and 34 points in his last 39 NHL games, then coached the Bruins to a 37–31–12 finish in 1985–86. He guided the team to a 7–5–1 mark in the first 13 games of 1986–87 before he was replaced. Name him.

23) Drafted first overall by the Bruins during the 1982 Entry Draft, this big defenceman (six foot four and 220 pounds) could never get on track because of knee injuries that required many surgeries. He was restricted to playing in only 229 games, although he did play in one Stanley Cup final series in 1988. His efforts to keep playing were recognized when he was awarded the Bill Masterton Trophy in 1990 for his dedication to hockey. Who was he?

24) The Bruins drafted this defenceman 166th overall in 1984 and he would go on to play 1,052 games for them between 1988 and 2003. He never scored more than seven goals in a season (and totalled 52 in his entire time in Boston), but he had double-digit assist totals for 12 straight seasons. He was signed as a free agent by the Dallas Stars in 2003. Name him.

25) When the Bruins traded Ray Bourque and Dave Andreychuk to Colorado on March 6, 2000, one of the players they received back was a centre who had played with New Jersey when the Devils won the Stanley Cup in 1995. He was a Devil until 2000, when he was dealt to Colorado, who then shipped him to Boston. As a Bruin, he had seasons of 19, 31 and 27 goals before he was lost as free agent to Minnesota in 2004. Who is he?

26) The Vancouver Canucks selected this tall (six-foot, three-inch) centre 42nd overall in 1994, and he also played with the New York Islanders, with whom he had seasons of 21 and 27 goals. The Bruins signed him as a free agent in 2005, but he only lasted 16 games in Boston before he was dealt to Phoenix for David Tanabe. Who is he?

27) He began his career with Boston in 1979–80 and scored 20 times for the Bruins in 1983–84, but was signed by Edmonton in 1985 and won three Stanley Cups with the Oilers. He was with the New York Rangers when they won the Cup in 1994 and coached the Oilers to the finals in 2006. Name him.

28) This native of Massachusetts was the first-ever captain of the Nashville Predators. He became a Bruin for the 2005–06 season (10 points in 71 games), his last in the NHL. He also played for the New York Islanders, Florida Panthers and Toronto Maple Leafs. Who was he?

DID YOU KNOW?

1) Which Boston player became the first Bruin to score four goals in one contest, against the Chicago Blackhawks on January 11, 1927? *Hint: He is a member of the Hall of Fame.*

2) On December 25, 1930, the Bruins hosted the Philadelphia Quakers, one of the worst teams in the history of the NHL. The Bruins ripped the Quakers by an 8–0 score and were led by a hat trick by one player. Who scored the three goals, and what happened during the game to get the Boston police involved?

3) He was the first coach in NHL history to pull his goalie for an extra attacker (during a playoff game in 1931), and was the Bruins' general manager for their first three Stanley Cup titles (in 1929, 1939 and 1941). Name him.

4) On March 19, 1936, the Bruins played the Toronto Maple Leafs to a 2–2 tie at Maple Leaf Gardens. What did Boston netminder

Tiny Thompson do that was a first for an NHL goalie?

5) March 4, 1944, saw the Bruins defeat the New York Rangers 10–9 in a high-scoring contest. What else was unusual about the game?

6) The Bruins set a team record on January 21, 1945, when they scored a club-record 14 goals in a 14–3 win on home ice. Against which team did the Bruins set their record?

7) This Hall of Fame player played his entire NHL career for the New York Rangers and then coached the Blueshirts for two seasons starting in 1948, but he became the Bruins' coach in 1950 and stayed in that position for

The Bruins plucked Ted Green (#6) from the Montreal organization and he recorded 1,029 penalty minutes in 620 career games with Boston.

four and half seasons. He took on the duties as general manager in 1953–54 and kept that role for 10 years. Who was he?

8) The Bruins did not have many great moments during the early 1960s, but on the night of January 18, 1964, Andy Hebenton and Dean Prentice each scored three goals as Boston defeated the Stanley Cup champion Maple Leafs in Toronto. What was the final score of the game?

9) On January 27, 1966, this Bruin centre scored four goals in one game as Boston beat Chicago 5–3. Who was the Boston sharpshooter on this night?
Hint: This player was later traded to Chicago.

10) On the final night of the 1965–66 season, the Bruins defeated the Chicago Blackhawks 4–2 at home to earn their 48th point of the year. Why was this victory significant?

11) When Bobby Orr became a Bruin he wanted to wear sweater number 2, as he had in junior hockey, but the number had been retired in honour of Eddie Shore, so Orr took number 27 instead. However, when another defenceman was cut from the team before the start of the season, Orr took his number 4 sweater because it was closer to number 2. Who was the player the Bruins let go, whose number Orr inherited?
Hint: He was a Stanley Cup winner with the Montreal Canadiens in 1958, 1959 and 1960.

12) Bobby Orr scored his first NHL goal on October 23, 1966, during a 3–2 loss at home to the Montreal Canadiens. Which Hall of Fame netminder gave up Orr's first goal?

13) On April 1, 1967, the last regular-season game of the "Original Six" era was played at Boston Garden. The Maple Leafs beat the Bruins 5–2, but the last goal of the game was scored by a Bruin right winger who tallied just his second marker of the season (in only eight games played). Can you name him?
Hint: He played parts of four seasons with the Bruins during the 1960s.

14) On January 19, 1971, Boston Garden hosted the NHL All-Star Game for the first and only time in its history. The West Division beat

Lynn Patrick played his entire 455-game NHL career with the New York Rangers and would go on to coach the Rangers, Bruins and Blues.

Ed Westfall was one of the better checking forwards on the Bruins during the 1960s and early '70s.

plateau, doing it in the next to last game of the season in Toronto. Who were the other 10 players?

17) March 1, 1984, saw the Bruins win their first regular-season overtime game since 1942. Boston beat Los Angeles 4–3 at home, and it was the Bruins' lone OT win of the entire 1983–84 season. Who scored the winning goal?

18) The Bruins acquired this centre, nicknamed "The Rat" for his over-the-edge style of play, from the Edmonton Oilers in exchange for Mike Krushelnyski on June 21, 1984. He stayed with Boston for five and half seasons, earning over 100 minutes in penalties four times. He was eventually traded to Philadelphia for a former Flyer captain. Name the player, and the one the Bruins received from the Flyers.

19) On February 7, 1992, the Bruins sent Stephane Quintal and Craig Janney to the St. Louis Blues in exchange for a high-scoring centre who would lead the NHL with 97 assists in 1992–93. Who was he?

20) This defenceman played in his 1,000th career game on December 9, 1992, with the Boston Bruins and although the Buffalo Sabres won the game 5–2, the blueliner became the first U.S.-born player to play in 1,000 NHL games. Who was this native of Detroit, Michigan? *Hint: He was with the Bruins for two seasons, 1992–93 and 1993–94.*

21) Ray Bourque played many great games for the Boston Bruins, and on February 8, 1993, he played in his 1,000th career game for the team when they lost to Pittsburgh 4–0. What was unusual about the location of the contest?

the East 2–1. A total of six Bruin players participated in the game, as did their coach. Can you name them all?

15) The Bruins were working quickly on the night of February 25, 1971, when they scored three goals in 20 seconds, going on to beat Vancouver 8–3 on home ice. Which three Bruins scored the goals?

16) The 1977–78 Bruins set an NHL record by having eleven 20-goal scorers on the team. Bob Miller was the last player to reach that

22) The Bruins and Canadiens played in the last playoff game ever held at the Montreal Forum. Boston won the game played on April 27, 1994, by a 3–2 margin, and the final goal was scored by a Bruin defenceman. Can you name him?

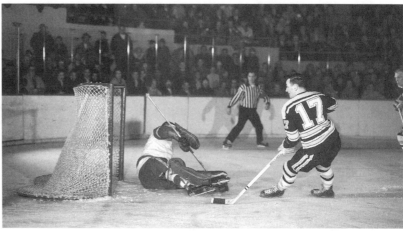

Dean Prentice (#17) joined the Bruins after a 1963 trade with the New York Rangers.

23) He won the Calder Trophy as the NHL's best rookie in 1997–98, when he scored 22 goals and 47 points in 81 games for the Bruins, who had drafted him eighth overall in the 1997 Entry Draft. Although the talented winger scored more than 20 goals in a season four times with the Bruins, he was dealt away to Edmonton during the 2005–06 season. Who is he?

24) After being named rookie of the year in 2004, goaltender Andrew Raycroft quickly fell out of favour in Boston and was dealt to Toronto in exchange for another goalie in 2006. Who is the top prospect the Bruins received from the Leafs?

25) Drafted 18th overall by the Bruins in 1991, this high-scoring right winger was dealt to Pittsburgh with Bryan Smolinski in return for Kevin Stevens and Shawn McEachern on August 2, 1995. He was re-acquired in a deal with Los Angeles in October of 2001, producing 30 or more goals in three consecutive years upon his return (44 was his single-season high, in 2002–03). He was still with the Bruins at the start of the 2006–07 season. Who is he?

26) A native of Flint, Michigan, this goaltender was originally drafted by Quebec in 1994, but he didn't play in the NHL until the Bruins signed him in 2002. He made four appearances for Boston in 2002–03, winning three times. The Bruins signed him as a free agent once again in 2005 and he played in 38 games in 2005–06, posting a 12–13–10 record, and became the team's number one goalie in 2006–07, winning 30 games. Who is he?

27) Drafted 209th overall by Boston in 2001, this netminder played all of one minute for the Bruins in 2005–06 and did not face a single shot on goal. He attended Bowling Green University and played most of 2005–06 with the Bruins' farm team in Providence, where he won 19 games. Who is he?

28) Named head coach of the Bruins prior to the start of the 2006–07 season, Dave Lewis was bench boss of one other NHL team previously. Name the team.

CHICAGO BLACKHAWKS

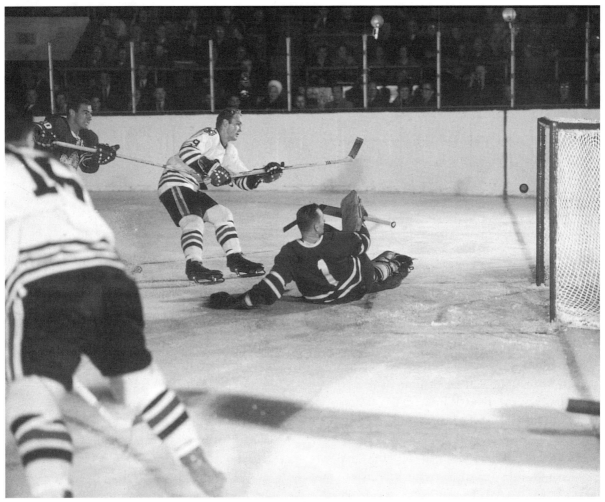

Chicago's Bobby Hull (#9) puts one past Toronto goaltender Johnny Bower.

MEMORABLE GAMES

1) Chicago Stadium was revered throughout its long history as one of the great buildings in which to watch a hockey game, and it all started on December 15, 1929, when the Blackhawks beat the visitors 3–1. Who was the visiting team that night?

2) On March 31, 1931, the Blackhawks played their first-ever overtime playoff game at home and beat the Toronto Maple Leafs 2–1. Who scored the winning goal after 19:20 of extra time at the Chicago Stadium?

3) The Blackhawks made it to the Stanley Cup finals for the first time in 1931 and hosted the first two games of the series against the Montreal Canadiens. The Habs won the opener 2–1, but Chicago rebounded to take the next game 2–1 in overtime on April 5, 1931. They also won the third game, 3–2 in overtime in Montreal, to take the series lead. Who scored the winning goals?

4) Chicago won the Stanley Cup for the first time in 1934, when they beat the Detroit Red Wings in the finals. They clinched the championship on April 10, 1934, at the Stadium with a 1–0 victory in overtime. Who scored the Cup-winning goal for the Blackhawks?

5) When the Blackhawks made it to the Stanley Cup finals in 1938, they were underdogs to the heavily favoured Toronto Maple Leafs. They were in even more trouble when regular netminder Mike Karakas was injured and unable to play the opening game. They were able to find a Toronto-area netminder to fill in

Chicago right winger Eric Nesterenko (#15) is watched closely by Toronto's Bob Baun.

for one game on April 5, 1938. Who was the goalie, and what was the result of his only playoff appearance?

6) Chicago won the Stanley Cup for the second time when they beat the Maple Leafs 4–1 on home ice on April 12, 1938. Who scored the Cup-winning goal?
Hint: This player would go on to be the NHL's referee-in-chief.

7) On April 13, 1944, the Blackhawks were on the verge of being eliminated by the Montreal Canadiens in the best-of-seven Stanley Cup final series. The Habs were looking to clinch the Cup on home ice, but the Blackhawks gave

them a battle before losing 5–4 in overtime on a goal by Toe Blake. Montreal netminder Bill Durnan also stopped the first-ever penalty shot taken in the finals. Who was the Chicago player he foiled?

8) This goaltender played a total of nine NHL games between 1925 and 1934 and did not play his 10th until he was 46 years old. By November 24, 1951, he was Chicago's team trainer when he was pressed into service by the Blackhawks after regular netminder Harry Lumley was injured. Who was he, and how did he fare?

9) The 1951–52 season was not a great one for the Blackhawks, who finished in last place with just 43 points during a 70-game schedule. However on the night of March 23, 1954, at New York's Madison Square Garden, a Chicago winger scored three goals in an NHL-record 21 seconds. Who was he, and who assisted on all three tallies?

10) During the 1953 semi-finals the Blackhawks nearly upset the Montreal Canadiens, although they ultimately lost in seven games. After Montreal took the first two games, Chicago responded with a 2–1 overtime triumph in the third game. Who scored the winner for the Blackhawks?

11) The night of November 25, 1954, saw this Blackhawk became the first Chicago

player to record 250 career goals when he scored against the Montreal Canadiens during a 3–2 loss. Who was he?

12) On October 22, 1957, this Blackhawk rookie scored his first NHL goal on home ice as Chicago beat Boston 2–1. Who was he?

13) This Chicago tough guy set an NHL record (which has since been broken) by recording 37 penalty minutes in one game versus the New York Rangers at Madison Square Garden. The Rangers won the game 2–0, but this player left his mark by recording a minor, three majors, a misconduct and a game misconduct. Can you name the Blackhawks' bad boy?

14) The Blackhawks made it to the Stanley Cup finals in 1961, ending the Montreal Canadiens' dynasty in the process, by winning their semi-final series against the Habs in six games. The most memorable game of the series was the

Left winger Ab McDonald (#14) was acquired in a trade with Montreal in 1960.

hard-fought third match, played on March 26 at Chicago Stadium, when the Blackhawks won 2–1 in double overtime. Who scored the game-winner for Chicago?

15) The Blackhawks won their third Stanley Cup on April 16, 1961, when they beat the Detroit Red Wings 5–1 and captured the championship in six games. Which Chicago player scored the Cup-winning goal?

16) As Stanley Cup champions, the Blackhawks hosted the NHL All-Star Game on October 7, 1961, and faced the best of the rest of the league. The NHL All-Stars beat Chicago 3–1. Which right winger, known primarily as a checker, scored the Blackhawks goal?

17) The first player from a team other than Montreal to score 50 goals in one season was Chicago's Bobby Hull, who scored his 50th on March 25, 1962, at Madison Square Garden. It was the only Blackhawk goal in a 4–1 loss to the Rangers. Who was the New York goalie?

18) In 1964 the Detroit Red Wings surprised the Blackhawks by eliminating them in a seven-game semi-final series. In 1965 Chicago returned the favour, knocking off Detroit in another seven-game tussle. They went on to play Montreal in the finals, and the series went the full seven games. It was a remarkable series in that the home team won every time. The last game was played on May 1 — marking the first time an NHL playoff game had been played in the month of May — at the Montreal Forum. What was the final score?

19) Chicago's Bobby Hull had been hoping to break Maurice Richard's record of 50 goals in

Bobby Hull was a perennial 50-goal scorer for the Blackhawks.

one season for some time, and he finally did it the night of March 12, 1966, when the Blackhawks faced the New York Rangers at home. Hull's bullet shot from the point finally found its way to the back of the net to give him 51 on the season. Which Ranger goalie let the historic puck get past him?

20) March 12, 1967, saw the Blackhawks accomplish something for the first time in their history when they beat the Maple Leafs 4–0 at home. What was the feat they achieved?

21) The 1969–70 season saw a Chicago rookie netminder record 15 shutouts to set a modern-day record. His final shutout of the season came on March 29, 1970, on home ice as the Blackhawks won the game 4–0. Who was the

goalie and which team did he blank for his final shutout?

22) Chicago beat Philadelphia in four straight games to start the 1971 playoffs, but they had a much more difficult time with the New York Rangers in the semi-finals. They won the series in seven games; in the fifth contest, at home on April 27, they beat New York 3–2 in overtime. Who scored the goal to give Chicago the series lead?

23) May 4, 1971, saw Chicago win the opening game of the Stanley Cup finals when they edged Montreal 2–1 in double overtime at the Stadium. Who scored for the Blackhawks to end a very long evening?

24) Chicago Stadium hosted its final NHL All-Star Game on January 19, 1991, in the midst of the Gulf War, and the fans roared their approval during the singing of "The Star-Spangled Banner" in support of the troops. The Campbell Conference won the game 11–5 over a Wales Conference team that featured three Blackhawk players. Can you name all of them?

25) The final game at Chicago Stadium was played on April 28, 1994. The Toronto Maple Leafs faced the Blackhawks in the sixth game of their first-round playoff series. What was the final score of the final contest?

26) The Blackhawks were thrilled to sign Stanley Cup–winning netminder Nikolai Khabibulin from Tampa Bay in August of 2005, and he won his first game for Chicago on October 7 of that year. Which team did he beat by a 6–3 score on home ice?

27) His debut with the Blackhawks was much anticipated by the team, and this winger did not disappoint, scoring two goals and adding two assists as Chicago beat Nashville 8–6 in the opening game of the 2006–07 campaign on October 5, 2006. Who is he?

28) On December 22, 2006, this player scored his 500th career goal as a member of the Blackhawks during a 3–1 Chicago victory over Toronto. Who is he?
Hint: This player was known as a Washington Capital for most of his career.

Goaltender Tony Esposito (#35) was acquired by Chicago from the Montreal Canadiens in 1969.

RECORDS AND AWARDS

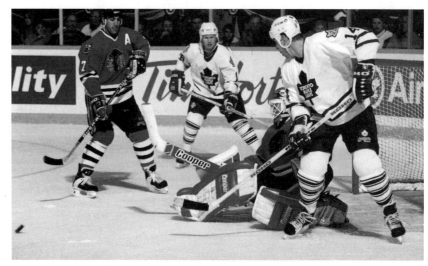

Defenceman Chris Chelios (#7) was picked up in a major trade with Montreal in 1990.

1) This native of Minneapolis, Minnesota, became Chicago's first major award winner when he got the Calder Trophy in 1938 as the NHL's best rookie. He topped off a great year (10 goals and 19 assists in 48 games) with a Stanley Cup win in 1938. He played his entire NHL career (342 games) with the Blackhawks. Can you name him?

2) He was the second NHL player to record five points in one period of a game, when he notched two goals and three assists in the second period of the Blackhawks' 8–1 drubbing of the Montreal Canadiens at Chicago Stadium on January 28, 1940. Who had the hot hand for Chicago that night?

3) The only brothers to win the Art Ross Trophy were both members of the Blackhawks during the 1940s. They formed two-thirds of the highly explosive Pony Line. Can you name them?

4) The Blackhawks finished the 1948–49 schedule in fifth place with a 21–31–8 record over the 60-game schedule. Despite this poor year, the Chicago club had the two leading point scorers in the NHL. Doug Bentley finished second with 66 points. Which of his teammates outproduced him by two points?

5) Even though he won only 12 games in 1953–54 for the last-place Chicago club, this goaltender was still awarded the Hart Trophy as the NHL's best player. Who was he?

6) Eddie Litzenberger was with Chicago in 1954–55, recording 51 points in 73 games played, when he was awarded the Calder Trophy as the NHL's top rookie. What was unusual about Litzenberger's season?

7) The Blackhawks became a much better team and organization when they lured this executive away from the Detroit Red Wings. He coached Chicago for a couple of seasons and was the general manager in 1961 when the Blackhawks won the Stanley Cup. In 1975 he was awarded the Lester Patrick Trophy for his outstanding service to hockey in the United States. Name him.

8) Named captain of the Blackhawks in 1961, this defenceman was an NHL All-Star (five times on the first team, three times on the second

squad) every year between 1960 and 1967. In addition, he won the Norris Trophy as the NHL's best defenceman three straight years, from 1963 to 1965. Who was he?

9) On November 7, 1962, this Blackhawk player suffered a pinched nerve in his back, forcing him out of the contest against the Boston Bruins. The game was the 502nd in a row that he had started for the Blackhawks. Who was this durable player?

10) He scored his first NHL goal on October 7, 1959, when he beat Gump Worsley of the New York Rangers and by the 1966–67 season, he led the NHL in points, winning the Art Ross Trophy. The slick Chicago centre also won the Hart Trophy and the Lady

Goaltender Al Rollins came to Chicago in a trade with the Maple Leafs.

Byng Trophy that same season and then repeated the feat for the 1967–68 campaign. Who was he?

11) A member of Chicago's famed Scooter Line, this right winger — who won the Lady Byng Trophy in 1964 — scored a goal just nine seconds into a playoff game against Toronto on April 9, 1967. Name him.

12) Bobby Hull scored his 604th and final goal as a Blackhawk on April 2, 1972, when the Blackhawks beat Detroit 6–1. Hull's mark still stands as the club record, and most of it was built with 50-goal seasons. How many times did Hull score 50 or more while he was with Chicago?
a) 4 b) 5 c) 6

13) On January 20, 1969, the Chicago Blackhawks set a club record for most goals in one game when they won 12–0. Which team did Chicago trounce to set the club mark?

14) A March 30, 1969, game between Chicago and Detroit saw this Blackhawk defenceman set a team record with six assists. Who was this stellar blueliner?

15) Bobby Hull became the first player to score 500 career goals for the Chicago Blackhawks when he hit the milestone on February 21, 1970. Which goalie allowed Hull's marker?

16) This Chicago coach won his 500th game (474 with the Blackhawks and 26 with the Maple Leafs) on April 7, 1975, in a 3–0 shutout of the Minnesota North Stars. It was also an important win for the team — the 1,200th in team history. Who was the Chicago coach in question?

17) Stan Mikita scored his 500th career goal on February 27, 1977, when the Blackhawks played the Vancouver Canucks. Which netminder allowed the goal?

18) When the Blackhawks signed this coach out of junior hockey for the 1982–83 season, they were very pleased with the results: Chicago posted a 47–23–10 record for 104 points. They also won one playoff series, but the coach suggested his players needed a heart transplant when they lost in the second round. He was awarded the Jack Adams Award in '83 but was gone less than two years later. Who was he?

19) A May 7, 1985, playoff game between Edmonton and Chicago produced an NHL record for the fastest three goals by two teams. The three tallies came in a 21-second span of the third period of the game, with Jari Kurri and Glenn Anderson scoring for the Oilers, while a Blackhawk defenceman got the other. Who was he?

20) The Frank J. Selke Trophy is given to the forward who excels at the defensive aspects of the game. Two Chicago players have won the award since its inception in 1978. Name both.

21) Only one Chicago goalie has ever won the William M. Jennings Trophy for allowing the fewest goals during a season. He did it twice, playing in so many games each time that the backup goalies didn't get their names on the award. Who was this durable netminder?

22) The Bill Masterton Trophy is awarded annually to the player who exemplifies the qualities of perseverance, sportsmanship and dedication to hockey. The first Chicago player

Pierre Pilote (#3) was captain of the Blackhawks between 1961 and 1968.

to receive this award was named the winner in 1970. Can you name him?

23) This smooth-skating centre holds the Chicago team record for most assists in one season (87 in 1981–82 and 1987–88) as well as the most points in a season by a centre (131 in 1987–88). He recorded his 1,000th career point as a Blackhawk on March 11, 1990, during a game against St. Louis. Who is he?

24) He holds the Chicago team record for most points by a rookie (90 in 1982–83, which earned him the Calder Trophy) as well as the team record for most consecutive games played (884 between October 1982 and April 1993). Name him.

25) How many times have the Blackhawks recorded 100 or more points in a season, and how many

times have they won the Presidents' Trophy for having the best overall mark in the NHL?

26) This blueliner was drafted first overall by the Ottawa Senators, but he never played a game for that team. He was traded to the New York Islanders and then, in the middle of his third season, to the Toronto Maple Leafs, with whom he suffered a very serious eye injury. He also played for the New York Rangers and Boston Bruins before the Blackhawks signed him as a free agent for the 2003–04 season. He had 47 points in 58 games for Chicago that year and won the Bill Masterton Trophy. Who is he?

27) This big defenceman was signed as a free agent by the Blackhawks after good seasons with Vancouver (23 goals in 1998–99) and the New York Islanders. He was named the 32nd captain in Chicago history on October 4, 2005. Name him.

28) Drafted 14th overall by Chicago after a junior career with Lethbridge of the WHL, this defenceman joined the Blackhawks for the 2005–06 season. He led all Chicago defencemen in points (32) in 2005–06 and had a plus/minus rating of plus-5 on the year. Who is he?

TRADES

1) Chicago acquired this future Hall of Fame player by sending defenceman Ted Graham to the Montreal Maroons in October of 1933. The defenceman the Blackhawks got back in the deal won the Stanley Cup with Chicago in 1933–34 while scoring 10 goals and 23 points during the regular season. He was traded away one year later. Who was he?

2) The hockey world was shocked when the Montreal Canadiens traded the legendary Howie Morenz to the Blackhawks on October 3, 1934. The Habs also sent Lorne Chabot and Marty Burke to Chicago to seal the deal. Which three players were sent to Montreal to complete the transaction?

3) A Minnesota-born left wing/centre, Elwyn "Doc" Romnes, first joined the Blackhawks in the 1930–31 season and won two Stanley Cups (1934 and 1938). He racked up double-digit goal totals in four different seasons with Chicago. He was dealt to Toronto early in the 1938–39 season. Who did the Blackhawks receive in return?

Goaltender Glenn Hall (#1) recorded 51 career shutouts with the Blackhawks.

4) Everyone remembers Emile "The Cat" Francis as a coach and general manager, but he got his start in the NHL as a goalkeeper with the Chicago Blackhawks in 1946. He played two years in Chicago before he was dealt to the New York Rangers in a trade that sent another goalie to the Blackhawks. Who was the netminder Chicago received?

Right winger Ken Wharram (#17) shoulders up to centre Danny Lewicki and left winger Ted Lindsay.

5) On August 20, 1951, the Blackhawks sent $75,000 and player Hugh Coflin to Detroit for six players, five of whom had been on the 1949 Red Wings team that won the Stanley Cup. Can you name all six players?

6) Hall of Fame defenceman Bill Gadsby began his career with Chicago in the 1946–47 season, and he stayed with the Blackhawks until November 23, 1954, when he was involved in a trade with the New York Rangers. Pete Conacher went with Gadsby to New York, and in return the Blackhawks received three players. Can you name all three?

7) During the 1956–57 season, goaltender Glenn Hall won 38 games for the Detroit Red Wings, but Detroit management decided to give the goaltending job back to Terry Sawchuk, who they re-acquired from Boston. The Blackhawks seized the moment, landing Hall and another player in a deal completed on July 23, 1957. Who came with Hall to Chicago, and who went to Detroit to complete the big swap?

8) On June 8, 1964, the Blackhawks sent Reggie Fleming and Ab McDonald to Boston for a left wing/defenceman who began his NHL career in 1953–54 with the Bruins. He would play the next six and half years with Chicago (scoring 20 or more goals four times) before he was dealt along with Terry Caffery to Minnesota in 1970–71 for Danny O'Shea. Who was he?

9) September 11, 1952, saw the Blackhawks acquire four players from the Toronto Maple Leafs in exchange for goaltender Harry Lumley. Who were the four sent to Chicago? *Hint: Three of the four were with the Leafs when they won the Stanley Cup in 1951.*

10) Goaltender Denis DeJordy began his NHL career with Chicago in 1962–63 and shared the Vezina Trophy with Glenn Hall during the 1966–67 season. He was dealt to Los Angeles

on February 20, 1970, along with Gilles Marotte and Jim Stanfield, for three players who all helped the Blackhawks get to the Stanley Cup finals in 1971. Name all three.

11) On September 9, 1971, the Blackhawks sent three players to the California Seals for a goaltender known as "Suitcase" because he had moved around so much during his career. Can you name all the players involved in the trade?

12) This defenceman was drafted second overall by Vancouver in 1970 but was traded to Chicago on May 14, 1973, for two players. The player Chicago received in the deal scored 15 goals twice for the Blackhawks and had a 62-point season in 1975–76. Can you name all the players exchanged in this swap?

Defenceman Pat Stapleton (#12) was an important member of Team Canada in 1972.

13) Darryl Maggs was drafted 48th overall by Chicago in 1969, but he never did impress enough to earn a spot on the team and was dealt away to the California Golden Seals on December 5, 1972. The Blackhawks got two players in return, one of whom turned out to be a good defenceman. Can you name both players?

14) Vancouver selected this native of Cornwall, Ontario, 22nd overall in the 1978 Entry Draft, and the left winger twice scored 25 or more goals for the Canucks, but he soon found himself in Chicago via a deal that saw Tony Tanti head to the west coast on January 6, 1983. Who did the Blackhawks receive?

15) After the Blackhawks acquired right winger Rick Vaive from Toronto in September of 1987, he scored 43 times in 1987–88. However, when Mike Keenan took over as coach he dealt Vaive to Buffalo on December 26, 1988. Who did the Sabres send to Chicago?

16) Chicago had high hopes for defenceman Dave Manson when they selected him 11th overall in the 1985 Entry Draft. The overly aggressive Manson scored 18 times in 1988–89 (with 352 minutes in penalties) and then had 14 tallies in 1990–91. But on October 2, 1991, he was dealt to Edmonton in exchange for another blueliner. Who was the player Chicago acquired?
Hint: The player Chicago received had won three Stanley Cups as an Oiler.

17) The outstanding goaltending career of Dominik Hasek actually started in Chicago during the 1990–91 season. He posted a 13–4–2 record as a Blackhawk, but Chicago already had Ed Belfour as their number one netminder, so Hasek was

dealt to the Buffalo Sabres. The Sabres sent Stephane Beauregard and a fourth-round draft choice to the Blackhawks in a deal completed on August 7, 1992. Who did Chicago take with the draft pick?

18) Selected 180th overall by Calgary in 1984, this high-scoring defenceman won the Calder Trophy in 1986 and a Stanley Cup with the Flames in 1989. He found his way to Chicago when the Blackhawks and Flames completed a swap on March 11, 1994. The skilled blueliner would record his third 20-goal season when he notched exactly 20 for the Blackhawks in 1995–96. Who was he, and who did Chicago send to the Flames?

19) Despite a long and illustrious career (406 goals scored between 1980 and 1993) with the Blackhawks, right winger Steve Larmer could not come to terms on a contract with Chicago, forcing a trade to the Hartford Whalers, who immediately flipped him to the New York Rangers, on November 2, 1993. Along with Larmer, the Blackhawks sent one other player to the Whalers and received two in return. Can you name the three other players in this deal?

20) Centre Jeremy Roenick was one of the best players Chicago has ever chosen in the first round of the NHL draft (eighth overall in 1988), and he played eight full seasons for the Blackhawks. Despite three 100-point seasons, Roenick was dealt away to the Phoenix Coyotes on August 16, 1996, in exchange for two players and a first-round draft pick. It was a poor deal for Chicago, who essentially got nothing for a very good player. Can you name the two players they

picked up, and who the draft choice turned out to be?

21) Even though he won three major awards while with Chicago and was an NHL first-team All-Star twice, goaltender Ed Belfour was dealt to the San Jose Sharks on January 25, 1997, in exchange for three players who did little for the Blackhawks. Who were they?

22) After scoring 19 goals for Chicago in 2002–03 and 22 goals in 2003–04, this centre looked as though he was going to have a good career with the Blackhawks. However, after scoring just 13 goals through 60 games in 2005–06, he was dealt to Ottawa on March 9, 2006, for an unproven talent in Brandon Bochenski. Who did Chicago trade away?

Right winger Dirk Graham (#33) was captain of the Blackhawks from 1988–89 to 1994–95.

he retired. In three of his seasons with the Blackhawks he did not score a single goal, but he did find the net once in the 1961 playoffs to help the team win the Stanley Cup. He went on to coach in California, Cleveland and Hartford. Who was he?

7) When he rumbled down the ice, Chicago fans would yell out "Mooooose" for this large defenceman (six foot two, 200 pounds) who first joined the team in 1956–57. He was twice named a second-team All-Star (1963 and 1964) and was a member of the 1961 Stanley Cup team. He recorded 20 or more points five times as a Blackhawk but would finish his career with a three-year stint with the Minnesota North Stars. Who was he?

8) He began his career by playing one game for the Blackhawks in the 1961 playoffs, which got his name engraved on the Stanley Cup for the only time in his career. He went on to play in 841 games for Chicago and recorded 435 points (including 143 goals) before his career ended after the 1975–76 season. His best playoff year was in 1971 when he had 11 points (six goals and five assists) in 18 games. Who was he?

9) Right winger Wayne Hicks was the only U.S.–born player (born in Aberdeen, Washington) on Chicago's Stanley Cup team of 1961. He got his name on the Cup by playing one game in the '61 playoffs, and he played just one regular-season game for the Blackhawks before he was dealt to the Montreal

Canadiens for a veteran defenceman. The blueliner who came to Chicago played four solid seasons (recording three years of more than 90 minutes in penalties) before he was reclaimed by the Canadiens. He also played for the Rangers and Penguins before he retired. Who was he?
Hint: He coached Montreal to the 1971 Stanley Cup when the Canadiens beat the Blackhawks in the finals.

10) A native of London, Ontario, this defenceman first joined the Blackhawks in 1964–65, when he had 17 points in 46 games played. He recorded 20 or more points five times with Chicago and he recorded 23 points in 99 playoff games. In all, he played 721 regular-season games and amassed 216 points with Chicago before he was dealt to the New York Rangers on October 28, 1975, in return for goalie Gilles Villemure. Who was he?

11) This goaltender was drafted 45th overall by Chicago in 1972, but he ended up being the backup netminder to Tony Esposito and would only win 20 games for the team. He was dealt to Hartford in 1980, where he played in

Chicago defenceman Lee Fogolin moves in to help goalie Harry Lumley against the Maple Leafs.

29 games in 1980–81, winning only six times. He also played with Winnipeg for part of his final year in the NHL. Can you name him?

12) Signed as a free agent by Chicago in 1969, this defenceman played 589 games as a Blackhawk and led the NHL in penalty minutes (1969–70 and 1970–71). He never scored more than two goals in a season but recorded 100 or more penalty minutes a total of seven times.

Chicago's Elmer "Moose" Vasko (#4) and Jack "Tex" Evans combine to stop Detroit's Norm Ullman.

Named team captain in 1976–77, he would go on to coach the Blackhawks for almost two seasons in the early 1980s. Who was he?

13) Chicago purchased the rights to this right winger from Los Angeles of the Western Hockey League in August of 1967 and it was one of the best investments the Blackhawks had ever made. He scored 20 or more goals five times for Chicago, including a 33-goal season in 1972–73. His entire 814-game career was played with the Blackhawks and he finished with 208 goals and 462 points. He played in the Stanley Cup finals in 1971 and 1973. Who was he?

14) This big left winger (six foot two, 200 pounds) was selected ninth overall by Chicago in 1968, and he played all of his 657 career games with the Blackhawks. He scored 21 goals twice in his time with Chicago, and he set a team record

by scoring two goals in 33 seconds from the start of a game (during a 5–5 tie versus Philadelphia on November 13, 1975). He ended his career with 112 goals and 275 points before retiring. Can you name him?

15) Selected 52nd overall by Chicago in 1974, this defenceman played his entire 1,008-game career with the Blackhawks. He showed a good offensive touch, recording 514 points, including 382 assists. He was team captain during the in 1985–86 season and would go on to be the Blackhawks' general manager in 1997–98 and 1998–99. Can you name him?

16) One of the better trades the Blackhawks made occurred on May 24, 1974, when they sent Len Frig and Mike Christie to the California Seals for a centre who would lead the team in goals scored three times. He also led the team in assists twice, and he led Chicago in points three times. In spite of this performance he

was dealt to Atlanta in 1979. Name him.
Hint: He was with Vancouver when the Canucks went to the Stanley Cup finals in 1982.

17) A member of the U.S. gold medal–winning Olympic team of 1980, this defenceman was selected 96th overall by Chicago in 1977. He joined the Blackhawks for the first of his five seasons in Chicago in 1982–83. His highest point total as a Blackhawk was 23 in 1985–86. The New Jersey Devils claimed him in the Waiver Draft of 1987. Who was he?

18) Selected second overall by Atlanta in 1972, this slick centre came to Chicago in a major deal that saw Pat Ribble, Miles Zaharko and Harold Phillipoff also join the Blackhawks after a trade was completed with the Flames on March 13, 1979. The centreman was by far the best player the Blackhawks received in the deal, and he would lead Chicago in assists (55) and points (76) in 1980–81. He had six seasons of 30 or more assists for Chicago before he retired after the 1985–86 season. Who was he?

19) Acquired in the trade that saw Pit Martin go to Vancouver, this goaltender played all but one of his 289 NHL games with Chicago. He won 20 or more games four times as a Blackhawk, including 27 in 1984–85. His 3.83 career goals-against average was not stellar (although he did play in the high-scoring 1980s), but he did post a 20–18 won/lost mark in the playoffs. Who was he?

20) Taken 179th overall by Chicago in the 1978 Entry Draft, this grinding left winger overcame the long odds to make a significant contribution. His first full year in the NHL saw him score 40

goals in 76 games during the 1980–81 campaign, and he enjoyed four more years of 20 or more goals. He was named captain of the team in 1982–83, but injuries brought an end to his playing days after the 1986–87 season. He returned to coach the Blackhawks for three seasons in the 1990s. Who is he?

21) Drafted seventh overall by Chicago in 1979, this defenceman would go on to play in 812 games as a Blackhawk before he was traded away in 1993. He recorded 20 or more points nine times with Chicago and had 36 points in 103 playoff games. After 14 years in Chicago he was dealt to the Florida Panthers for Darin Kimble. Who was he?

Goaltender Murray Bannerman took Chicago to the Campbell Conference Finals in 1982 (losing to Vancouver) and 1985 (losing to Edmonton).

Grinding forward Darryl Sutter scored 161 career goals for Chicago and also coached the Blackhawks for three seasons.

22) Signed as a free agent in 1989, this left winger would go on to set the Blackhawks' team record for most penalty minutes in one season when he had 408 in 1991–92 (a season that also saw him score six goals in 63 games played). He scored 15 goals for Ottawa in 1992–93 and went on to play for the New Jersey Devils when they won the Stanley Cup in 1995. Who was he?

23) After a long career with the Quebec Nordiques, this smooth left winger came to the Blackhawks in a trade completed on March 5, 1990. He scored 20 or more goals with Chicago three times and also recorded his 500th goal and 1,000th career point with the Blackhawks. He was elected to the Hall of Fame. Who was he?

24) Nicknamed "The Grim Reaper," this large (six foot four, 240 pounds) left winger became a Blackhawk when they claimed him on waivers from the Calgary Flames in 1990. The noted pugilist played three seasons with Chicago and scored a total of three goals, but managed to record 610 penalty minutes (including 234 in 1991–92) in 167 games played. He was claimed in the 1993 Expansion Draft by the Mighty Ducks of Anaheim in 1993. Can you name him?

25) After the Hawks plucked this small right winger off waivers from Toronto in 1999, he scored 34 goals and 75 points for Chicago in the 2000–01 season. He never had fewer than 60 points as a Blackhawk, and he would have surpassed that mark again in 2003–04 but he was traded after 56 games to the Nashville Predators on February 16, 2004. Who was he, and what did the Blackhawks receive in return?

26) He was named the 35th coach of the Blackhawks on July 7, 2005, and the former Chicago defenceman coached the team to a 26–43–13 record in 2005–06, then was replaced by Denis Savard early in the 2006–07 campaign. Who is he?

27) Known as one of the most vocal players in the NHL, this right winger was originally drafted by Buffalo (83rd overall in 1992) and had a career-high 19 goals for the Sabres in 1996–97. He also played for Pittsburgh, Tampa Bay, New York Rangers and Colorado before he joined the Blackhawks as a free agent in July of 2004. He played the 2005–06 season in Chicago, but managed just 28 points in 82 games — although he did record 178 penalty minutes. He then signed with the Dallas Stars. Name him.

28) Selected 90th overall by Chicago in 1993, this six-foot, six-inch, 235-pound right winger had many productive years with the Blackhawks (scoring at least 22 goals in eight straight seasons, including a high of 38) before a serious back injury derailed his career. Who is this native of Montreal, Quebec?

DID YOU KNOW?

1) Chicago owner Major Frederic McLaughlin liked the idea of icing a team made up completely of American-born players, but he could not find enough players that fit this description to fill out a complete roster. There were, however, eight U.S.–born players on the Chicago club that won the Stanley Cup in 1938. Can you name at least four of the them?

2) In addition to being the first U.S.–born coach to lead his team to a Stanley Cup title, with Chicago in 1938, this bench boss was also a major-league baseball umpire. Can you name him?

3) This left winger played in only 11 games as a Blackhawk, all of them during the 1942–43 season. He scored one goal (on January 3, 1943, in a 3–3 tie against the New York Rangers), on which he was assisted by his two brothers. Who was he?

4) Chicago team president Bill Tobin was one of the men responsible for organizing the very first NHL All-Star Game, played in Toronto in 1947. In return for his assistance it was decided that the second such game would be played in Chicago, even though the Maple Leafs, as Stanley Cup champions, would normally have

Chicago's Steve Sullivan keeps a close watch on Mats Sundin of Toronto.

hosted the game again. On November 3, 1948, the NHL All-Stars beat the Leafs 3–1 at the Stadium. Which Blackhawk players were on the All-Star team that night?
Hint: There are three players to be named.

5) A Hall of Fame player on the strength of his splendid play as a member of the Detroit Red Wings, his playing rights were purchased by the Blackhawks in July of 1952 with the idea that he would be a playing coach with Chicago. The 1952–53 season saw him get into 39 games (recording nine points), and the team made the playoffs with a 27–28–15 mark. He played in only three games the following season, in which the Blackhawks won just 12 games. He soon found

himself back in Detroit, where he was coach and general manager for many years. Who was he?

6) This former Blackhawk player (1926 to 1929) turned out to be one the greatest coaches in NHL history, winning Stanley Cups with Toronto and Montreal. He was hired to coach in Chicago for the 1955–56 season (a year that saw the Blackhawks go 19–39–12), but an illness forced him to retire. He won the final game he coached on March 18, 1956, when Chicago beat Boston 3–2. Who was he?

7) Chicago fans were so irate over the work of this referee during an April 4, 1959, playoff game against the Montreal Canadiens that at least one of the spectators tried to physically

Sid Abel began his coaching career with Chicago but won only 39 of 140 games.

attack him. The crowd was especially upset when a trip of Bobby Hull was supposedly missed. Montreal's Doug Harvey had to rescue the referee from the fans, but NHL president Clarence Campbell was not pleased with the ref's work. Who was the referee and what did he do after the game?

8) A native of Winnipeg, Manitoba, this coach was behind the Chicago bench for six full seasons between 1957 and 1962, posting a record of 162–151–74. He made the playoffs five times and won the Stanley Cup in 1961. Who was he?

9) The 1960–61 Chicago team that won the Stanley Cup featured a line nicknamed the Million-Dollar Line. Bobby Hull was one of the three members of this unit. The other two had come to the Blackhawks from the Montreal organization. Can you name both?

10) This native of Kirkland Lake, Ontario, began his NHL career with Chicago by playing one game in the 1961 Stanley Cup finals. He played three seasons as a low-scoring defenceman for the Blackhawks between 1961 and 1964, and was traded to the New York Rangers along with Doug Robinson and John Brenneman in a deal that netted the Blackhawks, among others, former rookie of the year Camille Henry on February 4, 1965. Who was the blueliner dealt to the Rangers?

11) The only time the Blackhawks faced the NHL All-Stars as a team occurred on October 7, 1961, at the Chicago Stadium as they opened the 1961–62 season as defending Stanley Cup champions. The All-Stars outshot the Blackhawks 35–23 and beat

Rudy Pilous won 162 career games as Chicago's head coach between 1957 and 1962.

them 3–1 before 14,534 fans. Who scored the lone Chicago goal?

12) To start the 1965–66 season, the Blackhawks played their first four games on the road (becoming the first NHL team to do so). What was Chicago's record during that road trip?

13) Picked up in a cash deal with the New York Rangers during the 1965–66 season, Chicago fans warmed up to this player, chanting "Looouuu" every time he touched the puck. He assisted on Bobby Hull's record-breaking 51st goal against the Rangers on March 12, 1966. He was claimed by the Philadelphia Flyers in the 1967 Expansion Draft, becoming their first captain, and later played for Pittsburgh. He returned to Chicago for four more years in 1969. Can you name him?

14) On March 18, 1967, Bobby Hull became the first player in NHL history to record two consecutive 50-goal seasons. He scored his 50th of the year during a 9–5 loss to the Maple Leafs in Toronto. Which Leaf netminder gave up the goal?

15) Bobby Hull scored 58 goals for Chicago in 1968–69. That Blackhawk team featured four players who scored exactly 30 goals each during the regular season. Can you name all four?

16) Drafted 16th overall by Chicago in 1974, this big right winger played all but 12 contests of his 586-game career as a Blackhawk. He scored a career-high 39 goals in 1979–80 and also had a 30-goal year in 1981–82. He holds the Chicago team record for most goals in one game with five, against St. Louis during a 9–5 Blackhawk win on home ice on February 2, 1982. Name him.

17) This superstar defenceman signed with Chicago as a free agent in 1976, but injuries limited him to only 26 games (totalling 27 points) over the course of two seasons. His final NHL goals came against goaltender Rogie Vachon of the Detroit Red Wings on October 28, 1978. Name him.

18) Drafted sixth overall by Chicago in 1977, this blueliner was the best-scoring defenceman in the history of the team. He played in 938 games for Chicago, recording 779 points (225 goals) and taking the Norris Trophy as the league's top defender in 1982. He was dealt to San Jose in 1991, and the Blackhawks got little in return. Who was he?

19) Besides Bobby Hull, which other Blackhawk players have scored 50 or more goals in one season?

20) He led the Blackhawks in points for seven straight seasons (1981–82 to 1987–88) and scored four goals in one playoff game against Toronto in 1986. In 2006–07 he took over as head coach of Chicago. Who is he?

Stan Mikita won three major trophies in 1967–68 and again in 1968–69.

21) As this goaltender warmed up before a game against the Canadiens at the Montreal Forum, Larry Robinson of the Habs approached one of the Blackhawks and inquired, "Where's the other half of your goalie?" He was referring to a netminder who stood five foot five and weighed 155 pounds. He would play in 81 games for Chicago and post a record of 27–35–7 between 1984 and 1989. He became a broadcaster after his playing days were over. Who was he?

22) This native of Chicago, Illinois, became a Blackhawk after a trade with the Montreal Canadiens in 1990, and he became the third Chicago defenceman to win the Norris Trophy when he took the award in 1993 and 1996. He was dealt to Detroit in 1999. Who is he?

23) A March 21, 1994, deal saw the Blackhawks send Brian Noonan and Stephane Matteau to the New York Rangers for this very swift right winger. He would go on to score 30 or more goals six times, and in three seasons he scored more than 40. Chicago let him go as a free agent in 2002 and he signed with Phoenix. Who is he?

24) Selected 12th overall by Chicago in 1992, this very talented Russian-born right winger could never get going in his six seasons as a Blackhawk (his highest goal total was 13 in 1996–97). He was traded to Nashville in 1998 for what were termed "future considerations." He scored 25 goals for the Predators in 1998–99 but was soon moved to Calgary. He also played with Minnesota and Anaheim. Who is he?

25) When the Blackhawks honoured Denis Savard by retiring his sweater number 18, it marked the fifth time Chicago has done this for a

player. Who are the other four, and what are their numbers?

26) This centre/left winger was selected 9th overall by Chicago in 2001 and he made his debut as a Blackhawk in 2003–04, when he scored 23 goals and 44 points in 82 games as an NHL rookie. He was tied with Kyle Calder for the team lead in power-play goals with 10 in 2003–04. Who is he?

27) Signed as a free agent by the Blackhawks in July of 2004, this left winger was named the top rookie in the American Hockey League for the 2004–05 season when he had 60 points in 78 games with Norfolk. He scored his first NHL goal in his first game as Blackhawk on October 5, 2005. Who is he?

28) Signed as a free agent by Chicago in July of 2006, this goaltender had a career record of 171–130–40 before he signed with the Blackhawks. He won 20 or more games five times in his career and had 33 shutouts. He was originally drafted by the Pittsburgh Penguins and posted a 4–6–1 record in 2006–07, with one shutout for Chicago. Who is he?

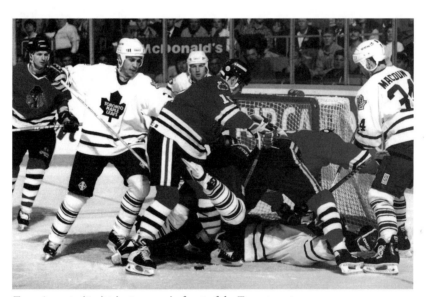

Tony Amonte (#10) tries to score in front of the Toronto net.

DETROIT RED WINGS

Gordie Howe was an NHL All-Star a remarkable 21 times (12 times on the first All-Star team) in 25 seasons as a Red Wing.

MEMORABLE GAMES

1) The longest playoff game in NHL history featured the Red Wings and the Montreal Maroons on March 24, 1936, at the Forum. Detroit won the game 1–0 on a goal scored after 116:30 of extra play (in the *sixth* overtime period). Who scored the game-winner?

2) April 7, 1936, saw the Red Wings become the first team to score nine goals in one playoff game when Detroit beat Toronto 9–4 in the second game of the Stanley Cup finals. One Detroit player scored two goals and added two assists in that contest. Who was he?

3) The Detroit Red Wings were the last of the "Original Six" teams to win the Stanley Cup when they did it at Maple Leaf Gardens on April 11, 1936, with a 3–2 win over the Maple Leafs. Who scored the Cup-winning goal?

4) This rookie Detroit goalie recorded shutouts in each of the last two games of the Stanley Cup finals by defeating the New York Rangers 1–0 on April 13, 1937, and 3–0 on April 15. Can you name this netminder?

5) This Detroit rookie scored three goals in 1:52 as the Red Wings beat Chicago 5–1 on March 13, 1938. Can you name him?

6) The night of March 23, 1939, saw this Red Wing forward set an NHL playoff record by scoring three power-play goals in one game when Detroit beat Montreal 7–3. Who scored the goals?

7) This Detroit player set an NHL record by recording seven assists in one game when the Red Wings beat Chicago 10–6 on March 16, 1947. The record has been equalled but never surpassed. Who was the Red Wing player who established the mark?

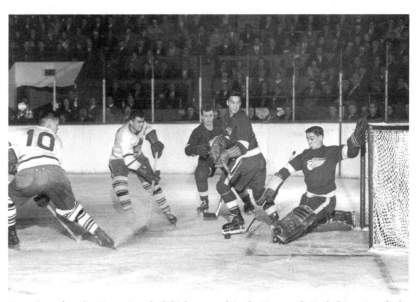

Detroit goaltender Terry Sawchuk kicks out a drive by Toronto's Tod Sloan. Sawchuk recorded 85 shutouts as a Red Wing.

8) After losing the Stanley Cup finals in 1941 and 1942, the Red Wings bounced back to win the championship by defeating the Bruins in four straight games. The final two games of the series were played in Boston, and this Detroit netminder shut out the Bruins 4–0 on April 7, 1943, and 2–0 on April 8. Can you name the Detroit goalie?

9) April 23, 1950, marked the first time the Stanley Cup finals were decided after a seventh game went into overtime. The Red Wings managed to edge the New York Rangers on a goal scored after 28:31 of extra time to give Detroit their fourth championship. Who scored the winner?

10) This Red Wing goalie closed the 1952 Stanley Cup finals with shutout wins (both by 3–0 scores) over the Montreal Canadiens on April 13 and April 15, 1952. Who was the netminder who took Detroit to a Cup win in eight straight games in the '52 playoffs?

11) Detroit won the Stanley Cup on April 16, 1954, when they beat Montreal in seven games. The Cup was won on an overtime winner at the Detroit Olympia, scored when a shot by a Red Wing forward bounced in off the glove of Canadiens defenceman Doug Harvey. Which Detroit player was credited with the winner?

12) The second game of the 1955 Stanley Cup finals saw one Detroit player score four goals during a 7–1 victory at the Olympia. Who notched the four tallies for the Red Wings?

13) The 1955 Stanley Cup finals went to seven games, with the Red Wings prevailing with a 3–1 victory on April 14. Which Detroit player scored the winning goal at the Olympia?

14) The Red Wings were underdogs to the Maple Leafs in the 1960 semi-finals, but they got a great deal of confidence by winning the fourth game of the series in Detroit. The Red Wings took the game played on March 29, 1960, by a score of 2–1 on an overtime marker scored by which player?

Red Wing Tony Leswick takes the puck to safety during a game against Toronto. Leswick was traded to Detroit by New York for Gaye Stewart.

15) November 10, 1963, was a special night for Gordie Howe, who set a new NHL record by scoring his 545th career goal, surpassing the mark held by Maurice Richard. Which Montreal netminder allowed the historic goal at the Detroit Olympia?

16) On January 18, 1964, Detroit beat Montreal 2–0 at the Montreal Forum. What was significant about that shutout?

17) The Red Wings nearly ended their Stanley Cup drought in 1964 when they met the Maple Leafs in the finals. They lost the series in seven games, but they did beat the Leafs 4–3 in overtime in the second game, played at Maple Leaf Gardens on April 14. Which Red Wing scored the winner?
Hint: He would be traded to the Leafs and would help Toronto to the 1967 Stanley Cup.

18) This veteran centre worked very fast on the night of April 11, 1965, scoring two goals for the Red Wings in just five seconds to set an NHL record, during a playoff game against the Chicago Blackhawks. Who scored the goals?

19) This player became the first Red Wing to take a penalty shot in the playoffs when he beat Allan Bester of Toronto on April 9, 1988, during a 6–3 win at Maple Leaf Gardens. Who scored the goal?

20) After being out of the playoffs since 1966, the Red Wings made it back to the post-season in 1970 but were quickly eliminated in four straight games. When Chicago beat them 4–2 in the final game of the series at the Olympia on April 12, 1970, what made the final score unusual?

21) After missing the playoffs every year from 1970–71 until 1976–77, the Red Wings made it back to the post-season in 1978 and won the best-of-three preliminary round series in two straight contests. Which team did the Red Wings eliminate?

22) When the Red Wings finally made it back to the Stanley Cup finals in 1995, they won the Western Conference finals by defeating the Blackhawks in five games. Detroit beat Chicago in overtime three times in the series: 2–1 on June 1, 4–3 on June 6 and 2–1 on June 11 to close out the series on home ice. Which three players scored the overtime goals?

23) On June 7, 1997, Detroit finally won the Stanley Cup for the first time since 1955. That night, they defeated Philadelphia 2–1 at Joe Louis Arena. Who scored the winning goal?

24) The Red Wings had a fairly easy time defeating the Washington Capitals in four straight games to win the Stanley Cup in 1998. The only contest that posed some difficulty was the second game of the series, played on June 11 at Joe Louis Arena. Detroit prevailed with a 5–4 overtime victory on a goal scored at 15:24 of extra time. Who scored the winner?

25) Even though the Red Wings lost the first game of the 2002 Stanley Cup finals in overtime to the Carolina Hurricanes on home ice, they rebounded to take the series in five games. Detroit's biggest victory came in the third game of the series on June 8 in Carolina, when they

Ted Lindsay is about to put the puck past Toronto netminder Harry Lumley.

recorded a 3–2 overtime win. It was a long extra session (54 minutes and 47 seconds), but the Red Wings prevailed on a goal scored by which player?

26) The Mighty Ducks of Anaheim met the Red Wings in the opening round of the 2003 playoffs and beat them in four straight games. The Ducks got off to a great start when they won the first game 2–1 at Joe Louis Arena on April 10. Which Duck scored the game-winner on Wings netminder Curtis Joseph?

Detroit defenceman Nicklas Lidstrom (#5) takes out Toronto winger Rob Pearson along the boards.

27) En route to the Stanley Cup finals in 2004, the Calgary Flames eliminated the Red Wings in the Western Conference semi-final. Two Flames scored game-winning goals in overtime, in the first and sixth games, respectively. Who are they?

28) The Red Wings were expected to have no problem defeating the Edmonton Oilers in the 2006 playoffs, but instead they lost the series in six games. Two of those games went into double overtime, with each team winning one. Who scored in overtime for Detroit in the first game, and for Edmonton in the third game?

RECORDS AND AWARDS

1) It was the most one-sided game in NHL history. On January 23, 1944, Detroit exploded for 15 unanswered goals. Which unfortunate team was on the receiving end of this 15–0 defeat?

2) The Detroit team record for most goals in one game by an individual player is six. On February 3, 1944, when the Red Wings whipped the New York Rangers 12–3, this Detroit winger became one of only seven players in NHL history to score six times in one game. Who was he?

3) In the same game, another Red Wing registered a team-record seven points (with a goal and six assists). He shares this distinction with Billy Taylor and Carl Liscombe. Who was he? *Hint: His nickname was "The Count."*

4) Although Detroit lost the 1966 Stanley Cup finals to Montreal, this Red Wing was nevertheless a very deserving winner of the prestigious Conn Smythe Trophy, presented to the best player in the playoffs. Who was he?

5) The Norris Trophy, recognizing the best defenceman in the NHL, was first awarded in 1954 and a Red Wing blueliner was its first-ever recipient. He scored 16 goals and added 33 assists for 49 points in 62 games played during the 1953–54 season. Who was he?

6) Between December 13, 1956, and November 11, 1964, this longtime Red Wing star did not miss a single game. He was also the team captain for more than 10 years and coached the club in the 1970s. Who was he?

7) Five different Detroit goalies have recorded 10 or more shutouts in one season, but only two of them have recorded 12 in a season at least once. Name the two netminders.

8) Known as a bad boy throughout his NHL career, this Red Wing defenceman led the NHL in penalty minutes with 273 in 1962–63. He played parts of five seasons with Detroit and recorded over 100 penalty minutes four times. Who was he?

9) He was the last Red Wing player to lead the NHL in goals scored during the regular season, with 42 during the 1964–65 season. Who was he?
Hint: He was traded to Toronto in 1968.

10) True or false: Gordie Howe is the only Detroit Red Wing to win the Art Ross Trophy as the NHL's regular-season point leader.

11) Besides Gordie Howe, how many Red Wings have won the Hart Trophy as the NHL's most valuable player?
a) 2 b) 3 c) 4

12) Gordie Howe was the first player in NHL history to score 700 career goals. He reached that plateau when the Red Wings beat the Pittsburgh Penguins 7–2 on December 4, 1968. Which Penguin netminder gave up the milestone goal?

13) On March 13, 1985, Edmonton netminder Grant Fuhr gave up a milestone goal to this Red Wing who became only the second Detroit player to score 50 or more in a season. Who was the high-scoring winger?
Hint: He also holds the Red Wing team record for most points in a season by a left winger with 105 (55G, 50A) in 1984–85.

14) This right winger was the first Detroit player to score 50 goals in a season when he scored

Red Wing blueliner Vladimir Konstantinov (#16) clears the front of the Detroit net.

against Toronto on March 27, 1973, during an 8–1 victory. Who scored the goal, and which Leaf goalie gave it up?

15) Although his stay in Detroit was not a happy one, this Hall of Fame centre did win the Lady Byng Trophy for the Red Wings during the 1974–75 season. Who was he?

16) This Hall of Fame defenceman finished his highly successful career with a two-year stint as a Detroit Red Wing. In 1983–84 he scored five goals and added 53 assists in 80 games and was awarded the Bill Masterton Trophy for his dedication to hockey. Who was he?

Red Wing Norm Ullman defends the Detroit net in front of netminder Glenn Hall.

17) Steve Yzerman scored 50 or more goals five times during his illustrious career with the Red Wings. Can you name all five goalies who gave up his 50th goal during those seasons?

18) An original draft choice of the Red Wings (46th overall in 1983), this tough but troubled winger would go on to set the Detroit team record for most career penalty minutes (2,090) as well as the single-season mark with 398 minutes in 1987–88. Who was he?

19) Terry Sawchuk set an NHL record by recording 103 career shutouts, and he holds the Detroit team record with 85. Which netminder is next on the Red Wings' all-time list for most career shutouts?

20) Although the 1995–96 Detroit club did not win the Stanley Cup, this edition of the Red Wings set a significant NHL record during the regular season. What was that mark?

21) This player scored his 500th NHL goal in a Detroit uniform on January 8, 1994, when he beat Kelly Hrudey of the Los Angeles Kings during a 6–3 Red Wings road victory. Who scored the milestone goal?
Hint: He began his NHL career with the Minnesota North Stars.

22) Since 1986 the NHL has given out the Presidents' Trophy to the team with the best record during the regular season. How many times have the Red Wings taken the award?

23) The Jack Adams Award has been presented to the best coach in the NHL since the 1973–74 season. Three different Detroit coaches have won it at least once. Can you name all three?

24) Four Red Wing players have been named the winner of the Conn Smythe Trophy as the best performer in the Stanley Cup playoffs. Can you name the players and the years they took the coveted award?

25) How many players have recorded their 1,000th career point as a Red Wing?
a) 5 b) 6 c) 7

26) The 2005–06 Red Wings set an NHL single-season record by winning 12 straight road games between March 1 and April 15, 2006. Which team did Detroit beat in the first and last games of the streak?

27) Drafted 187th overall in 1998, this Russian-born centre was on the Detroit team that won the Stanley Cup in 2002 (contributing six points in 21 playoff games). He also won the Lady Byng Trophy in 2005–06, when he led the Red Wings with 87 points (28 goals, 57 assists). Who is he?

28) Selected 210th overall by the Red Wings in 1999, this Swedish-born left winger was named rookie of the year in his native country in 2001 and then made the NHL's All-Rookie Team in 2003, when he had 22 goals and 44 points in the 2002–03 season. He led the Red Wings in goals scored with 39 in 2005–06 and 33 in 2006–07. Name him.

TRADES

1) On October 27, 1934, the Red Wings made a major acquisition, sending defenceman Burr Williams to the St. Louis Eagles for a netminder who would win a Vezina Trophy and a berth on the NHL's first All-Star team in 1936–37. He also helped Detroit win their first two Stanley Cups (1936 and '37). Who was this goalie?

2) In August of 1946 the Red Wings acquired Roy Conacher by trading one of their better players of the 1940s to the Boston Bruins. The player had been with Detroit for six seasons (between 1940 and '46) and scored 20 or more goals twice. He was on Detroit's championship team of 1943 (scoring a playoff-high six goals) and later returned to the Red Wings (via a trade with Montreal) and was on their Stanley Cup team of 1950. Who was he?

Pavel Datsyuk led the Red Wings in scoring with 87 points in 2006–07.

Detroit's Darren McCarty (#25) scored 19 goals for the Red Wings in 1996–97.

3) Bob Goldham was one of the best shot-blocking defencemen in NHL history, and he was picked up by the Red Wings in a trade with the Chicago Blackhawks completed on July 13, 1950. It was a good deal for Detroit, as Goldham anchored the Red Wing defence through three Stanley Cup wins. Who did Detroit send to Chicago?

4) Gaye Stewart had always been a good goal-scoring forward with Toronto and Chicago, and he scored 18 times for the Red Wings in 1950–51, but he was dealt to the New York Rangers on June 8, 1951. The trade saw Detroit pick up a winger who would play on three Stanley Cup teams for the Red Wings. Who was he?

5) One of the best trades in Red Wings history took place on June 12, 1961, when they sent minor-leaguer Les Hunt and cash to the New York Rangers for a defenceman who would be elected to the Hall of Fame. Who was he? *Hint: This player went on to coach the Red Wings in the 1968–69 season.*

6) A June 5, 1962, deal saw the Red Wings send Johnny McKenzie and Len Lunde to the Chicago Blackhawks for this defenceman who would finish as the runner-up for the Calder Trophy as the NHL's best rookie in 1962–63. In 1963–64 he scored 11 goals and totalled 32 points in 67 games. Who was he? *Hint: His career was cut short after a serious eye injury in 1966.*

7) The Chicago Blackhawks were looking to add toughness to their lineup when they acquired defenceman Howie Young from the Red Wings on June 5, 1963. Detroit got two players in return, one of them a goalie who would be named the NHL's rookie of the year in 1965. Can you name both players?

8) On February 16, 1966, the Red Wings sought some veteran help to solidify their defence after an injury to one of their regular blueliners. They made a deal with Boston, acquiring a future Hall of Fame player along with another veteran forward. Who were the two players Detroit picked up in the deal, and which three players did they send to Boston?

9) When the Buffalo Sabres joined the NHL in the 1970–71 season, they knew they needed a

quality goaltender to anchor their team. Sabres general manager Punch Imlach acquired Roger Crozier from the Red Wings on June 10, 1970, sending this forward to Detroit in return. Who was he?
Hint: He scored 30 goals and totalled 67 points for the Red Wings in 1970–71, his only full year in the NHL.

10) The Red Wings were quite pleased to pick up centre Garry Unger from Toronto in 1968, and he performed well for Detroit, especially in 1969–70 when he scored 42 goals. However, after 51 games the following season, Unger and veteran Wayne Connelly were dealt to the St. Louis Blues for two players. Who were they?

11) When the Red Wings dealt youngsters Don Luce and Mike Robitaille to the Sabres on May 25, 1971, it did not seem as though they had given up too much. However, both players would be with the Sabres when they went to the Stanley Cup finals in 1975. Who did the Red Wings receive in return?

12) Despite four great seasons as a Red Wing (including 121 points in 1974–75), centre Marcel Dionne wanted out of Detroit and signed as a free agent with the Los Angeles Kings. After a bitter dispute over the compensation the Red Wings were entitled to receive, a deal was worked out whereby Dionne and Bart Crashley would go to the Kings in exchange for

two players and a second-round draft choice. Who were the players Detroit received in return for their superstar?

13) Selected first overall by the Washington Capitals in 1974, defenceman Greg Joly joined the Red Wings after a deal was completed on November 30, 1976. Joly never lived up to his high draft status, but he did play more than seven seasons in Detroit and recorded a career-high 27 points (seven goals, 20 assists) in 1977–78. Who did Detroit give up to get Joly?

14) Right winger Mike Foligno was selected third overall by Detroit in the 1979 Entry Draft and had two very good years with the Red Wings, scoring 36 goals in his first year and 28 in his second. However, he was involved in one of the biggest deals in Red Wings history when he and two others were traded to Buffalo on December 2, 1981. Who were all the other players involved in this big trade?

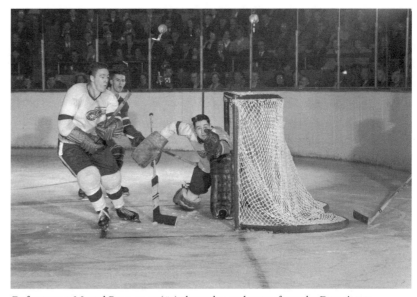

Defenceman Marcel Pronovost (#3) clears the puck away from the Detroit net occupied by netminder Glenn Hall.

15) Darryl Sittler thought he was about to be named captain of the Philadelphia Flyers, but instead he was dealt to the Red Wings on October 10, 1984. Detroit sent two players to the Flyers, helping Philadelphia make it to the Stanley Cup finals in 1985. Name both of them.

16) Detroit was the fifth organization the well-travelled Brent Ashton played for, but he was on the move again when the Red Wings sent him to Winnipeg for Paul MacLean in June of 1988. MacLean scored 36 goals and recorded 71 points in 1988–89, but he was dealt along with Adam Oates to the St. Louis Blues on June 15, 1989, for two players. Who did the Red Wings receive in return?

17) A native of Southfield, Michigan, centre Jimmy Carson did not like playing for the Edmonton Oilers and actively sought a trade. The Red Wings were very interested and acquired the high-scoring Carson (55 goals for Los Angeles in 1987–88) along with Kevin McClelland in return for four players on November 2, 1989. Who were the four sent to Edmonton?

18) Signed as a free agent, right winger Ray Sheppard proved to be an excellent acquisition when he scored 52 goals for the Red Wings in 1993–94. Sheppard was dealt to the San Jose Sharks on October 24, 1995, in return for a centre who would play on three Stanley Cup teams with Detroit. Who was he?

19) When Jimmy Carson did not work out well as a Red Wing, he was one of the principals in a trade to the Los Angeles Kings on January 29, 1993. Who else did the Red Wings send to the Kings, and who was the main player Detroit received in return?

20) The Red Wings were tired of seeing their talented team lose in the playoffs because of deficient goaltending, and so they made a trade on June 29, 1994, to acquire the very experienced (and one-time Stanley Cup winner) Mike Vernon from the Calgary Flames. Who did Detroit send to Calgary to complete the deal?

21) It was an unheralded deal when it was made on March 20, 1996, but the Red Wings picked up a useful player in Kirk Maltby, who would help them win three Stanley Cups in a mostly

Sergei Fedorov (#91) was a very valuable player for the Red Wings during the Stanley Cup wins of 1997, 1998 and 2002.

checking role. Who did Detroit send to Edmonton to complete the deal?

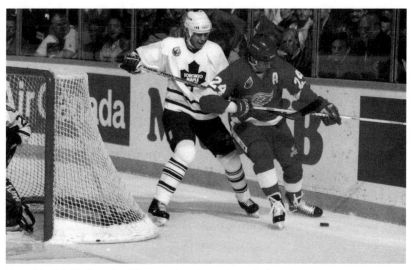

Detroit's Bob Probert (#24) has good position along the boards.

22) One of the best trades in Red Wings history was made when they acquired Brendan Shanahan from the Hartford Whalers on October 9, 1996. Detroit sent two players, plus a first-round draft choice (in 1997), east to Hartford to complete the deal. Who were the two players who left Detroit, and who else became a Red Wing in the deal?

23) The opportunity to acquire Norris Trophy–winning defenceman Chris Chelios was too much for the Red Wings to pass up, and they were willing to part with two first-round draft choices (in 1999 and 2001) plus a defenceman. Who was the blueliner the Wings sent to Chicago on March 23, 1999? *Hint: He was on Detroit's Stanley Cup–winning team of 1998.*

24) Prior to the start of the 2001–02 season, the Red Wings were looking to improve their goaltending, and six-time Vezina Trophy winner Dominik Hasek was available from the Buffalo Sabres. The deal was completed on July 1, 2001, and saw the Red Wings send one player plus a 2002 first-round draft choice to Buffalo. Who was the player?

25) This centre was originally drafted by Winnipeg in 1989 but only played 20 career games as a Jet (scoring three goals). The Red Wings acquired

him for future considerations in June 1993 and won three Stanley Cups. As of the end of the 2006–07 season, he had played 865 games as a Red Wing, scoring a total of 129 goals. Who is he?

26) One of the few Red Wing defencemen ever to score 20 or more goals in a season, this blueliner notched 21 in 2005–06. He was acquired by the Red Wings in a March 2003 deal with the Los Angeles Kings that saw them give up Sean Avery, Maxim Kuznetsov and two high draft choices. He also played for Montreal, the New York Islanders, Toronto and the New York Rangers. Who is he?

27) Acquired in a deal completed on February 27, 2004, that saw Detroit give up a first-round draft choice in 2004 and a fourth-round selection in 2005, this centre scored 20 goals and recorded 62 points in his first full season with the Red Wings. He has also played for Los Angeles, Boston, Pittsburgh and Washington. Who is he?

28) Detroit acquired this rugged right winger —
one of the most controversial players in recent
NHL history — at the trade deadline in 2007
by giving the Florida Panthers prospect Shawn
Matthias and two conditional draft choices.
Who did the Red Wings receive in return?

REMEMBER HIM?

1) A small right winger at five feet, six inches and
148 pounds, this player began his career with
Detroit in 1927–28, when the team was known
as the Cougars. He remained with the team
through two name changes (to the Falcons
and Red Wings), and the 1936–37 season saw

Detroit's Steve Yzerman (#19) battles Toronto's Doug
Gilmour in the face-off circle.

him lead the NHL in goals scored with 23. In
all, he reached double digits in goals scored in
10 straight seasons. He was on two Stanley
Cup teams (in 1936 and '37) and had 279
points in 489 career games — all played in a
Detroit uniform. Who was he?

2) On February 2, 1927, Detroit spent $4,000
to acquire this centre from Saskatoon. He
scored 25 goals and totalled 48 points in
1929–30 for the Detroit Falcons, but he had
his greatest success when he was switched to
defence in 1935–36 with the Red Wings.
He earned two selections to the first All-Star
team (1937 and 1940) and won the Hart
Trophy in 1940. The native of Ottawa,
Ontario, was on three Stanley Cup teams with
Detroit and was elected to the Hall of Fame.
Can you name him?

3) A native of Calgary, Alberta, this left winger
was acquired from Duluth of the American
Hockey Association in 1928. He scored 20
goals in 44 games for the Detroit Falcons in
1929–30, a feat he repeated in 1932–33 with the
Red Wings. He scored a total of 148 goals for
Detroit, recording 309 points in 483 games. He
was on two Stanley Cup teams as a Red Wing
(1936 and 1937) and his performance earned
him a spot in the Hockey Hall of Fame. Who
was he?

4) A July 11, 1935, trade saw the Red Wings deal
Cooney Weiland and Walt Bruswell to Boston
for Art Giroux and a high-scoring centre who
had scored 20 or more goals for the Bruins five
times. He would go on to lead the Red Wings
in scoring a total of three times while helping
the team win the Stanley Cup in 1936 and 1937.
In 1936–37 he recorded 44 points in 47 games

and won the Lady Byng Trophy. He was also a first-team All-Star in 1937 and would be elected to the Hall of Fame. Who was he?

5) The Red Wings acquired this big defenceman (six feet, 205 pounds) after completing a deal with Chicago early in the 1946–47 season. He spent the next six seasons in Detroit, helping the team win the Stanley Cup in 1950 and 1952. Never a high goal scorer, he nonetheless potted two overtime winners during the 1950 playoffs to help Detroit get past defending champion Toronto. His highest point total was 21 (a mark he reached twice while he was with Detroit). He was dealt to the Rangers in the summer of 1952. Who was he?

6) This native of Belfast, Ireland, joined the Red Wings for four playoff games in 1947 (recording two assists). He was a regular with the team in 1947–48, scoring 24 goals and 24 assists and winning the Calder Trophy. Although he was on the Stanley Cup team of 1950, he was never again as good for the Red Wings as in that first season. He had a 23-goal season with Chicago in 1952–53 but was gone from the NHL two years later. Who was he?

7) This native of Kitchener, Ontario, joined the Red Wings for the 1953–54 season and promptly scored 15 goals and added 33 assists in 69 regular-season games. The rookie centre

Red Wing defenceman Bob Goldham helps goaltender Terry Sawchuk defend against Toronto's George Armstrong and Harry Watson.

also got his name on the Stanley Cup that year, then scored 25 times and totalled 66 points in 70 games during the 1954–55 campaign. He was a strong performer in the '55 playoffs, with 12 points in 11 games, and won a second championship. His point totals dropped off after his first two years and he went on to play for Chicago and Boston, but was not in the NHL beyond the 1958–59 season. Who was he? *Hint: His nickname was "Dutch" and he recorded four assists in his first NHL game (a 4–1 Detroit win over New York on October 8, 1953).*

8) This right winger joined the Red Wings as a rookie during the 1953–54 season and scored 17 goals in 70 regular-season games. He was with the Red Wings for two Stanley Cup wins (1954 and '55), but would never score more than 12 goals in any one season for the rest of his playing career. He was dealt to Chicago, where he played most of his final NHL season in 1957–58. His three sons, Gord, Kevin and

Peter, all played in the NHL, and he coached in the World Hockey Association and in the NHL with Philadelphia. Who is he?

9) This left winger from Sault Ste. Marie, Ontario, joined the Red Wings for the 1947–48 season and would go on to play in 634 career games — all for Detroit. A member of three Stanley Cup teams (1950, 1954 and 1955), he never scored more than 17 goals in one season and finished with 252 points (93G, 159A). He retired after the 1956–57 season. Name him.

10) This Hall of Fame coach began working behind the Detroit bench during the 1947–48 season and never won fewer than 30 games in a season. He took the Red Wings to three championships and on two occasions won 44 games (in a 70-game schedule) and recorded over 100 points twice. Eventually he left for Chicago, where he coached and later became the general manager of the Blackhawks. Who was he?

11) He was named coach of the Red Wings for the 1954–55 season and won the Stanley Cup after posting a 42–17–11 record during the regular season. Although his overall record as Detroit coach was 123–78–46, he was replaced during the 1957–58 season when the Red Wings got off to a 13–17–7 start. Despite his good record, he never coached in the NHL again. Who was he?

12) A native of Edmonton, Alberta, this right winger began his career as a Red Wing during the 1960–61 season when he played 12 games during the season and eight playoff games, including appearances in the Stanley Cup finals against Chicago. He would also appear in the finals in 1963, 1964 and 1966 with Detroit, but he never won a Cup. He had a career-high 28 goals for Detroit in 1966–67 and recorded a total of 335 points as a Red Wing. He was traded to the New York Rangers in 1971 and helped his new team get to the finals in 1972. Name him.

13) A defenceman who was claimed by the Red Wings from the Montreal organization in the Intra-League Draft of 1964, he would go on to play 706 career games for Detroit. He was generally a low-scoring rearguard, but he did record 30 or more points six times and was with Detroit when they made the Stanley Cup finals in 1966. He was also known for his solid

Gary Doak (#24) of the Red Wings tries to keep Toronto's Red Kelly from getting to the puck.

Defenceman Jim Schoenfeld (#2) was a Red Wing for just two seasons.

play for Canada during the 1972 Summit Series versus the Soviet national team. Who was he?

14) Detroit picked up this veteran who had played for the Maple Leafs and Rangers in the Intra-League Draft of 1960, and he would go on to have his best seasons with the Red Wings. He scored 33 times in 1962–63 and 21 the following season. The five-foot, 11-inch, 160-pound native of Sydney, Nova Scotia, helped Detroit to the Stanley Cup finals twice (1963 and 1964). He was dealt to Boston in the summer of 1965, only to be re-acquired in a deal completed December 30, 1965, that saw Detroit give up a good young forward in Pit Martin. Who was he?

15) This left winger first joined the Detroit club in the 1967–68 season after a stellar junior career

with the Hamilton Red Wings of the Ontario Hockey Association. He scored 20 or more goals six times, including a career-high 31 in 1971–72. The native of Stratford, Ontario, was named one of many captains the team had in 1973–74. In 1979 he was dealt to the Pittsburgh Penguins, with whom he spent the final two years of his career. He finished with 217 goals as a Red Wing. Can you name him?

16) This goaltender joined the Red Wings in 1970–71 but was lost to the Pittsburgh Penguins in the Intra-League Draft of 1971. Detroit wanted him back and sent Ron Stackhouse to the Penguins to complete the deal. The smallish netminder (five foot eight, 168 pounds) would twice win 20 games for the Red Wings, but he posted only one winning season (20–17–4 in 1977–78) during his time in Detroit. He was traded to Toronto for Mark Kirton, and he also played for Los Angeles, but he played his final NHL game for Detroit. Who is he?
Hint: He would go on to be the general manager of a Stanley Cup–winning team.

17) Drafted 22nd overall in 1976 by the Red Wings, this native of Minnesota was one of the NHL's most underrated defencemen. He scored 20 or more goals in five straight years with Detroit and never had fewer than 17 as a Red Wing. He also recorded 100 or more penalty minutes seven times as a Red Wing, but found time to record 570 points for Detroit. He was dealt to Boston for Mike O'Connell on March 10, 1986. Who was he?

18) Taken 107th overall by Detroit in 1981, this feisty left winger scored 207 career goals as a Red Wing and recorded over 200 penalty

minutes four times. His best year was in 1988–89, when he recorded 93 points (39 goals, 54 assists) for the Red Wings and earned a spot on the NHL's second All-Star team. He signed as a free agent with the Tampa Bay Lightning in 1993, but played in only 51 games for them before retiring. Who was he?

19) Detroit selected this left wing/centre seventh overall in 1984, and he would go on to play in 659 games as a Red Wing while accumulating 362 points (including 214 assists). His best season in Detroit saw him score 24 goals and add 32 assists in 1989–90. He was traded to Tampa Bay and also played for the San Jose Sharks before he retired. Who was he?

20) Best known as one the top Russian players of all time, this Hall of Fame defenceman became a Red Wing after he had played more than five seasons with the New Jersey Devils. He was with Detroit for two Stanley Cups in 1997 and 1998. His best statistical year with Detroit came in 1995–96, when he had a total of 42 points. Who was this blueliner?

21) This noted tough guy was originally drafted by Detroit (91st overall) in 1983. He led the NHL in penalty minutes in 1985–86 with 377, and he recorded 200 or more penalty minutes in six seasons as a Red Wing. However, he also found time to score 16 goals and notch 36 points in 1989–90. He was traded to the New York Rangers, with whom he won a Stanley Cup in 1994. He returned to Detroit and won two Cups there to close out his career. Who was he?

22) Detroit's first choice (10th overall) in the 1991 Entry Draft was a right winger who had played junior hockey for Laval in the Quebec Major

Junior Hockey League. He won two Stanley Cups with Detroit, but didn't score more than 16 goals in a season with them until 2000–01, when he potted 27. In the summer of 2001, he signed a lucrative contract with the Boston Bruins. Who is he?

23) One of the greatest goal scorers in the history of the NHL (741 career markers), he scored a controversial Stanley Cup–winning goal for Dallas in 1999. He signed with Detroit as a free agent in 2001 and scored a playoff-leading 10 goals during the 2002 playoffs, which saw the Red Wings win the Cup. He also had a 37-goal season for Detroit in 2002–03. Name him.

Vyacheslav Kozlov (#13) scored 202 goals as a Red Wing.

Keith Primeau (#55) was drafted third overall by the Red Wings in 1990.

24) This defenceman (and sometime right winger) was drafted 49th overall in 1994 by the Red Wings after he played junior hockey for Sherbrooke in the QMJHL. He was a full-time member of the Detroit club by the 1996–97 season, a year that saw the Red Wings win the Stanley Cup. He was on two more championship clubs with the Red Wings. His best year in Detroit, 2000–01, saw him score 10 goals and total 25 points. He signed as a free agent with the Montreal Canadiens in 2005. Who is he?

25) The Red Wings picked up this netminder as a free agent in August of 1999, and he served primarily as the backup for his first three years in Detroit. He was with the team when they won the Stanley Cup in 2002 (going 10–6–2 in the regular season) and then played 41 games in 2003–04, posting a 23–10–5 record. He was the number one goalie in 2005–06 and won 37 games, but a first-round ouster from the playoffs sealed his fate as a Red Wing. He signed as a free agent with St. Louis in 2006. Who is he?

26) After nearly taking the Maple Leafs to the Stanley Cup finals in 2002, this netminder signed with the defending Cup champion Red Wings for the 2002–03 season, winning 34 games but getting wiped out in four straight playoff games. He was forced to share the goaltending duties with the returning Dominik Hasek the following season, but was let go after the lockout year of 2004–05. He signed as a free agent with Phoenix. Who is he?

27) He played in 1,431 career NHL games with Los Angeles, Pittsburgh, New York Rangers and Detroit, scoring 668 goals and 1,394 points. He joined the Red Wings as a free agent in July of 2001 and was with the team when they won the Stanley Cup in 2002 — the only championship of his career. Who was he? *Hint: His sweater number 20 was retired by the Kings in 2006.*

28) Drafted 25th overall in 1998, this big defenceman (six foot five, 225 pounds) played in 80 games in 2001–02 when the Red Wings won the Stanley Cup. He chipped in with six points in 22 playoff games in '02 and had 60 points in 305 career games before he was forced to retire after suffering a heart seizure on the Detroit bench during a game versus Nashville on November 21, 2005. Who was he?

DID YOU KNOW?

1) He first became Detroit's coach in 1927–28 and was behind the bench for 20 seasons, winning 413 games and losing 390 in 964 contests. He stopped coaching after the 1946–47 season to become general manager of the team, a job he held until 1962. Who was he?

2) November 10, 1932, saw the Detroit team wear their new uniforms with the now-famous winged-wheel emblem for the first time after they changed their nickname from Falcons. How did the newly christened Red Wings fare in their first contest?

3) This defenceman took over as the Red Wings' captain to start the 1935–36 season, the first year Detroit won the Stanley Cup. He also wore the coveted "C" on his sweater the next year, when the team repeated as champions. He scored 35 goals and had 80 points in 388 career games — all played in Detroit. Who was he?

4) This Red Wing defenceman recorded five points (a goal and four assists) in a playoff game on the night of April 9, 1942, during a 5–2 win over the Maple Leafs. Who was he?
Hint: He would go on to coach the Detroit's junior affiliate in Hamilton of the OHA after his career was over.

5) This left winger from Hamilton, Ontario, played in only one NHL game, and it was for the Red Wings during the 1950 Stanley Cup finals. He did not record a point, nor did he get a penalty, but his name is engraved on the Cup because he appeared in that one contest. Who was he?

Red Wing defenceman Leo Reise (wearing the "A" on his sweater) helps goaltender Harry Lumley defend against the New York Rangers in the 1950 Stanley Cup finals.

6) A March 10, 1948, contest between Detroit and Chicago (won by Detroit, 7–2) saw this Red Wing netminder become the first goalie in team history to record 30 wins in one season. Who was he?
Hint: He led the NHL in wins twice (34 in 1948–49 and 33 in 1949–50) while he was a Red Wing.

7) This goaltender from Fort William, Ontario, filled in for an injured Terry Sawchuk for three games early in the 1953–54 season and

posted a 2–0–1 record with a shutout (a 4–0 whitewash of Toronto on October 11, 1953) in his first-ever NHL game. He never played in the NHL again. Can you name him?

8) On December 25, 1956, Gordie Howe set a personal best for most points in one game when Detroit beat New York by a score of 8–1. How many points did Howe record in the game?
a) 5 b) 6 c) 7

9) During the 1956 semi-final playoff series between Toronto and Detroit, two Red Wing players were threatened with physical harm by a crazed fan if they showed up to Maple Leaf Gardens on March 24, 1956. Not only did they play, but Detroit won the contest 5–4 in overtime, and one of the targeted players got the winner. Who were the two players and which one netted the winner?

10) The Red Wings acquired this winger from the New York Rangers in August of 1955, and he played for the Red Wings until the 1956–57 season, when he scored 15 goals and added 15 assists. He scored four goals for Detroit the next season, the final one coming on November 28, 1957, before he was dealt to Chicago in December of the same year. He returned to Detroit for the 1969–70 season and scored 10 goals, the first of

which came on November 8, 1969. That marker meant that he had gone 11 years, 11 months and 11 days in between goals scored as a Red Wing. Who was he?
Hint: He also coached the Red Wings for exactly 100 games in two different stints between 1975 and 1982.

11) One of the largest in-season trades in NHL history took place on December 17, 1957, when Detroit sent Bill Dineen, Billy Dea, Lorne Ferguson and Earl Reibel to Chicago in exchange for four players. Can you name all four players the Red Wings received in return?

12) A November 27, 1960, contest between Toronto and Detroit saw Gordie Howe achieve a milestone that no other player had ever accomplished. What was the mark Howe hit during the 2–0 Red Wing victory?

13) This left winger from Wetaskiwin, Alberta, played seven seasons for the Red Wings between 1959 and 1967, recording 83 points in 375 games played. He recorded only 18 penalty

Detroit's Bill Dineen (#17) reaches out to swat at the puck in front of the Toronto net.

minutes with Detroit and played his last 87 games as a Red Wing without drawing a single penalty. Who was he?

14) Very few NHL players have come from this province, but this native of Bishop's Falls, Newfoundland, joined the Red Wings for 70 games during the 1962–63 season, scoring 10 goals and adding 10 assists. In the '63 post-season he scored five times (including two in one game against Toronto in the finals) in eight games. He recorded 12 points in 30 games during the 1963–64 season and played one game in the Stanley Cup finals, but never played in the NHL again. Who was he?

15) This former rookie of the year (1969 with Minnesota) became a Red Wing in August of 1974 and went on to score 50 goals and total 87 points for Detroit during the 1974–75 season. He was named team captain in 1975 (sharing the honour with Terry Harper for one year and Dennis Polonich for another), but he only scored 14 more goals the rest of his time in Detroit. He was dealt to Los Angeles in 1978. Name him.

16) This Red Wing centre got Detroit off to a great start on January 28, 1973, when he scored a goal after just six seconds of play during a 4–2 victory at the Montreal Forum. He was a Red Wing for three seasons before he was traded to Minnesota. Who was he?

17) Only two brothers have ever coached the Detroit Red Wings, and both did it during the decade of the 1970s. Can you name them? *Hint: Both also played for the Red Wings and each was on a Stanley Cup team with Detroit.*

Bruce MacGregor had 28 goals for the Red Wings in 1966–67.

18) Known more for his coaching career than his playing days, this right winger scored four goals in one game for the Red Wings on March 18, 1976, during a 6–3 win over the St. Louis Blues. He scored 32 times for Detroit in 1975–76 and had 21 the following year, but was dealt to the New York Islanders for Andre St. Laurent. Can you name him?

19) There was a time when the NHL avoided all contact with the upstart World Hockey Association, but on November 18, 1977, the Red Wings made an in-season deal with the Birmingham Bulls of the rival circuit. Detroit loaned the Bulls Dave Hanson and Steve Durbano and included future considerations in return for Tim Sheehy and a big Czech-born

centre who was an international hockey star. The six-foot-two, 205-pound pivot scored 38 goals for the Red Wings in 1978–79 and 35 the following year. Who was he?

20) The final game played at the Detroit Olympia took place on December 15, 1979, and the visitors were the Quebec Nordiques. What was the final score, and who scored the last goal in the Olympia?

21) Who was the last player to wear sweater number 19 prior to Steve Yzerman, and who was the last captain of the Red Wings prior to Yzerman?

Defenceman Gary Bergman was a member of Team Canada in 1972.

Henrik Zetterberg led Detroit with 33 goals in 2006–07.

22) Drafted 148th overall by Detroit in 1986, this defenceman from Peterborough, Ontario, played in only one NHL game — scoring a goal in Detroit's 10–7 loss to the Calgary Flames on October 5, 1989. He would go on to become an NHL referee. Who is he?

23) Since the universal draft began in 1969, the Detroit Red Wings have selected first overall on two occasions — 1977 and 1986. Who did Detroit take with the number one choice in each year?

24) Coach Scotty Bowman achieved many milestones during his long and distinguished career. One of those special moments came behind the Red Wing bench on February 8,

1997, when Detroit beat Pittsburgh 6–5. What milestone did Bowman achieve that night?

25) On October 26, 1997, Detroit beat Vancouver 5–1 and Steve Yzerman entered the record book when he became the longest-serving captain, wearing the "C" on his jersey for 11 years and 12 games. Whose record did he surpass?

Detroit goaltender Harry Lumley makes a save off a drive by Toronto forward Howie Meeker (#11).

26) Taken 257th overall by Detroit in 1994, this native of Sweden first joined the Red Wings for the 1996–97 season. He won the first of three Stanley Cups that season. The six-foot, 200-pound left winger had his best year in 2005–06, when he had 59 points (29G, 30A, and a plus/minus rating of plus-14). Name him.

27) When he left the head coaching position of the Anaheim Ducks, it seemed as though he might be out of work for a while, but he was hired by the Red Wings for the 2005–06 season and promptly won 58 games — the second-best mark in team history. Who is the coach in question?

Gordie Howe of Detroit uses his size against Toronto defenceman Hugh Bolton in front of the Maple Leafs' net.

28) Selected 13th overall by Chicago in 1997, this right winger soon found himself dealt to Edmonton in 1999. After four seasons as an Oiler, he signed as a free agent with Phoenix but was cut loose once again. Detroit signed the former junior all-star (with Belleville of the OHL), and he scored 20 goals for Detroit in 2006–07. Who is he?

MONTREAL CANADIENS

Maurice "Rocket" Richard was the greatest player in the history of the Montreal Canadiens.

MEMORABLE GAMES

1) On December 19, 1917, the Canadiens played their first game in the newly formed National Hockey League, defeating the Ottawa Senators 7–4. Who scored five goals for the Canadiens in that historic contest?

2) This Canadiens goaltender recorded the first shutout in NHL history when Montreal whipped the Toronto Arenas by a 9–0 score on February 18, 1918. Who was he?

3) January 10, 1920, saw the Canadiens play their first-ever game at the Mount Royal Arena, hosting the Toronto St. Patricks. Who won the

Jean Beliveau holds up the Stanley Cup, won at the Montreal Forum in 1965.

game, and which player scored six goals in the contest?

4) On March 3, 1920, the Canadiens set an NHL record that has yet to be equalled during their game against the Quebec Bulldogs. What was that mark?

5) During this Stanley Cup final game played on March 22, 1924, this Canadiens rookie scored three times and then notched the game-winner three days later to seal the championship. Who scored these important goals, and against which team?

6) Even though the Montreal Forum was not originally built for the Canadiens, they ended up playing the first game in the new building on November 29, 1924, winning the game 7–1. Who scored the first goal at the Forum, and which team did the Habs beat?

7) The Canadiens won their second straight Stanley Cup on April 5, 1931, when they beat the Chicago Blackhawks 2–0 in the final game of the best-of-five series, played in Montreal. Who scored the winning goal, and who earned the shutout?

8) Anyone who attended the playoff game between the Canadiens and Maple Leafs could never forget the five-goal performance of Maurice "Rocket" Richard on March 23, 1944. The Habs won the game 5–1 and went on to take the Stanley Cup. Which Leaf goalie allowed all five of Richard's goals, and what happened after the game?

9) Maurice Richard spent most of the day on December 28, 1944, moving into his new

Claude Provost was one of the top checkers in the league when he played in the NHL.

11) This Montreal netminder made his playoff debut in Chicago on the night of April 4, 1953, with the Habs badly in need of a win. The Blackhawks were on the verge of eliminating the Canadiens with a 3–2 lead in the series. Not only did the Habs win the game, but the new goalie also earned a shutout in the 3–0 win. Who was the goalie?

12) The night of April 16, 1953, saw the Canadiens clinch the Stanley Cup on home ice with a 1–0 overtime win over the Boston Bruins. Which Canadiens player scored the OT winner, and what netminder shut out the Bruins?

13) Lorne "Gump" Worsley had many rough nights when he played in net for the New York Rangers, and one such occasion came on February 19, 1955, when the Canadiens beat his team 10–2 at the Forum. One Montreal player scored five times that night. Who was he?

14) On November 5, 1955, this Montreal player scored three power-play goals in 44 seconds (players had to serve their entire penalty at the time) with the Boston Bruins down two men. Who scored the goals, and which Canadiens player assisted on all three in Montreal's 4–2 win over the Bruins?

15) A November 1, 1959, contest at Madison Square Garden saw Montreal netminder Jacques Plante put on a face mask for the first time during a game against the New York Rangers. Plante told coach Toe Blake he would not return to play the game after taking stitches in the face after stopping a shot. Blake objected but eventually relented and history was made with Montreal winning the game

home. But that night, he played for the Canadiens at the Forum and recorded eight points against the Detroit Red Wings. Which Detroit goalie faced the Rocket's onslaught in the Canadiens 9–1 victory?

10) The 1952 semi-final series between Montreal and Boston was decided during a seventh-game showdown at the Montreal Forum the night of April 8. The Habs won a tight contest 2–1 on an overtime marker by a player who had earlier been knocked out of the game after a violent collision. Who scored the goal in what was termed "a semi-conscious state?"

3–1. Which Ranger player struck Plante in the face with a backhand drive to start the chain of events that would change the face of hockey?

16) This Montreal right winger had the biggest goal-scoring night of any player in the decade of the 1960s when he notched five against the Detroit Red Wings on February 1, 1964. Who scored the goals, and which goalie gave them up?

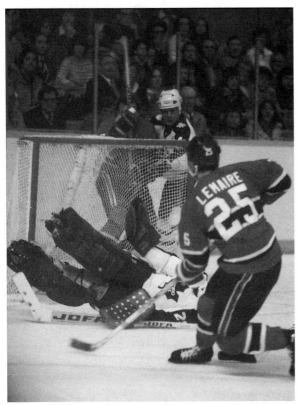

Jacques Lemaire (#25) scored many big goals for the Canadiens over his playing career.

17) The Maple Leafs had won three consecutive Stanley Cups in 1962, 1963 and 1964 and were looking for a fourth when they were eliminated by an overtime goal scored by Montreal on April 13, 1965. The goal was scored at Maple Leaf Gardens, with the Leafs looking to send the semi-final series back to Montreal for a seventh game. Who scored this dramatic goal?

18) May 1, 1965, saw the Canadiens reclaim the Stanley Cup with a 4–0 victory over the Blackhawks at the Montreal Forum. A goal just 14 seconds into the contest seemed to settle the issue quickly, and the player who notched the important marker was also named winner of the Conn Smythe Trophy. Who was he, and which goalie earned the shutout for the Habs?

19) On May 5, 1966, the Habs retained the Stanley Cup when they beat the Red Wings 3–2 during the sixth game of the finals at the Detroit Olympia. The winning goal came in overtime, and in controversial fashion, as it went in off the arm of this Montreal player who was sliding into the Red Wings' net. Who scored the goal?

20) It looked as if the Canadiens were going to lose the seventh game of the 1971 Stanley Cup finals, when Chicago took a 2–0 lead in the second period. But the Habs tied it before the middle stanza was over and then won the game in the third period on a goal by Henri Richard. Which two players scored the first two Montreal goals to get the game turned around?

21) On February 15, 1975, this Canadiens winger had the best goal-scoring night of his career when he poured in five past Chicago netminder Mike Veisor during a 12–3 win by Montreal at the Forum. Who was this Hab?

22) New Year's Eve 1975 saw one of the most memorable games ever played at the Forum

Ken Dryden came up late in the regular season and played a key role for the Canadiens in the 1971 playoffs.

when the Canadiens battled the Soviet Red Army team to a 3–3 tie — a game the Habs should have won easily, given their dominance throughout the contest. Who scored the Montreal goals, beating stubborn Soviet netminder Vladislav Tretiak in the process?

23) On May 16, 1976, the Canadiens put the finishing touch on their four-game sweep of the Philadelphia Flyers in the Stanley Cup finals with a 5–3 victory. Who scored the Cup-winning tally?

24) On June 3, 1993, the Canadiens nearly went down two games to none against the Los Angeles Kings in the Stanley Cup finals, but they scored late in regulation time to tie the game 2–2 and then won it in overtime. Who scored the winner for the Habs, and what was unusual about his performance that night?

25) On March 11, 1996, the final NHL game was played at the fabled Montreal Forum. Who did the Canadiens play that night, and which Hab scored the last goal at the legendary old arena?

26) The first game in which the Canadiens took part in a shootout came on the road against Pittsburgh on November 10, 2005. The shootout ended on a spectacular goal scored by one of the Penguins against netminder Jose Theodore. Who scored the goal for the winners?

27) This Czech-born centre first joined the Canadiens after a trade with the Washington Capitals in March of 2001. He didn't have his first 20-goal season until 2005–06. He had a big night on the road in Philadelphia on January 25, 2006, when he scored four goals as Montreal beat the Flyers 5–3. Who is he? *Hint: He signed with Vancouver for the 2006–07 season.*

28) When Montreal met the Carolina Hurricanes in the first round of the 2006 playoffs, three of the games went into overtime before the Hurricanes took the series four games to two. The Canadiens won one of the overtime games on the road, while Carolina won the other two (including the series-clinching game) in Montreal. Can you name all three OT goal scorers?

RECORDS AND AWARDS

1) The longest game involving the Canadiens occurred on March 28, 1930, when the New York Rangers visited the Forum for a playoff game. The contest was knotted at 1–1 and wasn't settled until 68:32 of extra time had been played, on a winning goal scored by a Montreal player. Who ended the longest game in Habs history?

2) The longest road game the Canadiens have ever played in the playoffs occurred on March 27, 1951, when Montreal edged Detroit 3–2 after 61:09 of extra time. Which Hab player scored the winner at the Detroit Olympia to give Montreal a 1–0 lead in the semi-final series?

3) March 18, 1945, was the final night of the 1944–45 season, and the Canadiens were visiting Boston for their last game. One member of the team was gunning for his 50th goal of the year in the 50th game of the season — trying to become the first NHL player to hit the magic number. He scored the goal by beating Bruin netminder Harvey Bennett. Who set a new standard for all NHL players that night?

4) History was made at the Montreal Forum on the night of October 30, 1957, when this Canadiens player scored his 500th career goal — becoming the first-ever NHL player to hit this milestone number. Who was he, and which goalie gave up the goal?

5) On April 14, 1960, the Canadiens clinched their fifth consecutive Stanley Cup with a 4–0 win in Toronto. In addition to setting a new precedent by winning five titles in a row, the '60 Canadiens tied another mark that was set by the Detroit Red Wings in 1952. What record did the Habs equal?

6) Which goaltender holds the Canadiens' team record for most career shutouts?
a) George Hainsworth b) Bill Durnan c) Jacques Plante d) Ken Dryden

7) Montreal netminders have had a long history of capturing the Vezina Trophy as the best goalies in the NHL. Prior to 1982, the award was given to the goaltender(s) on the team that allowed the fewest goals during the regular season. Two Montreal netminders captured the award a total of six times each. Can you name both?

8) During the 1950s, two Montreal players won the Calder Trophy for being the best first-year player in the NHL. Name both and the years they won the award.

Maurice Richard is checked closely by Toronto defenceman Marc Reaume.

Acquired in a deal with Los Angeles, goaltender Cristobal Huet was born in France.

12) This Montreal goalie finally got a chance to be the number one netminder for the 1963–64 season, and he made the most of his opportunity by winning the Vezina Trophy. He also shared the Vezina with a teammate in 1965–66. Who is he, and with whom did he share the Vezina in 1965–66?

13) Defenceman Gary Bergman faced the wrath of this Canadien player on the night of December 7, 1967, when he had three fouls committed against him in one play. Bergman was charged, high-sticked and slashed in the same sequence. Which Montreal player was given the first triple minor in NHL history?

Serge Savard (#18) was the first defenceman to win the Conn Smythe Trophy.

9) During the 1960s, two Montreal players won the Calder Trophy as the NHL's best rookies. Name both, and the years they won.

10) How many times has a Canadien won the Conn Smythe Trophy as the best player in the Stanley Cup playoffs? Can you name all the winners?

11) When the Canadiens won the Stanley Cup in five consecutive seasons between 1956 and 1960, they had five different players score the championship-clinching goals. Can you name all five players and the years they scored the Cup winners?

14) The Canadiens' team record for most points in one playoff year is held by a player acquired in a deal with the Detroit Red Wings. In 1971 he scored 14 goals and added 13 assists for 27 points. Can you name him?

15) Guy Lafleur was the first Canadien to record 100 points in a season when he recorded 119 points in 1974–75. A teammate hit the century mark in points in the same season, becoming just the second Montreal player to hit that mark. Who was he?
Hint: He was a centre acquired in a deal with the Detroit Red Wings.

16) The 1976–77 edition of the Montreal Canadiens was one of the best teams of all time, and they set an NHL record for most points earned in one season. How many points did they gain in 1976–77?
a) 100 b) 110 c) 120 d) 132

17) The Lester B. Pearson Trophy is given annually to the best player in the NHL as voted by his peers. Only one Montreal player has ever won this award, and he did it for three straight seasons. Who was he?

18) Four players have recorded their 1,000th career point as members of the Montreal Canadiens. Name all of them
Hint: All four are also the only Hab players to record their 500th goal in a Montreal uniform.

19) Which Montreal players scored the Stanley Cup–winning goals in 1977, 1978 and 1979?

20) Only five Montreal defenceman have won the Norris Trophy as the NHL's best blueliner. One Canadiens rearguard won the award a

total of six times, while another took the trophy twice. Can you name all five winners?

21) On May 18, 1986, in the second game of the Stanley Cup finals, the Canadiens set a record for the fastest game-winning goal in overtime when this forward scored after just nine seconds of extra play to give Montreal a 3–2 victory. Who was this fast worker?

22) Doug Harvey was the first Montreal defenceman to record five assists in one game when he accomplished the feat on March 19, 1955, during a 10–2 win over the New York Rangers. Which Hab defenceman repeated this achievement nearly 39 years later on February 2, 1994, when the Canadiens beat Hartford 9–2?

Bob Gainey was captain of the Canadiens between 1981 and 1989.

Peter Mahovlich (#20) was one of the more colourful Canadiens during his stay in Montreal.

23) Two Montreal goalies have won the Hart Trophy, awarded to the NHL's most valuable player. Name both goalies and the years they took the coveted award.

24) He began his NHL career with the Canadiens on October 8, 1975, and played a total of 560 consecutive games for the Habs (winning four Stanley Cups) before he was dealt to Washington. He also played with Hartford before his streak ended at an NHL-record 964 consecutive games. Who is he?
Hint: He was an assistant coach with Montreal in 2006–07.

25) These two are the only Canadien players ever to win the Frank J. Selke Trophy as best

defensive forwards in the NHL. In 2006–07, these same individuals were the general manager and coach of the Canadiens respectively. Who are they?

26) This low-scoring but hard-working forward first came to the Canadiens when they picked him up on waivers from Buffalo in October of 2003. He had his best year in 2005–06, when he had 23 points (11 goals, 12 assists) and also led Montreal forwards in blocked shots, getting in front of 64 opposition drives. Who is he?

27) The Canadiens already have a lengthy list of players who have had their sweater numbers retired. Two more Montreal greats were so honoured during the 2006–07 season. Can you name the two players and their sweater numbers? *Hint: Both are Hall of Fame players.*

28) Two former Montreal Canadiens were inducted to the Hockey Hall of Fame in 2006. One was a goalie and the other was a left winger, and both played on Stanley Cup winners with the Habs as well as with other NHL teams. Name both.

TRADES

1) Newsy Lalonde was one of the Canadiens' first stars (124 goals and 165 points in 98 games played) but he was dealt to the Saskatoon Sheiks on September 18, 1922. In return, the Habs acquired one of their best players of all time, who would go on to score 270 goals for them. Who was he?

2) Acquired from the Montreal Maroons on February 13, 1936, this centre played and later

coached the Canadiens with great success. He was with the Canadiens organization until he passed away. All the Habs sent to the Maroons was a netminder at the end of his career who would play in only 16 games for the Maroons. Who was the player the Canadiens received in the deal, and which goalie did they send to the Maroons?

3) A September 10, 1936, trade saw the Canadiens acquire a defenceman who had played with the Montreal Maroons, New York Rangers and Boston Bruins. The Habs sent two players to the Bruins to complete the deal and also received Roger Jenkins in the transaction. The blueliner would be named the NHL's most valuable player for the 1936–37 season. Who was he?

4) On September 11, 1945, the Canadiens sent Ray Getliffe, Roly Rossignol and the rights to Fern Gauthier to the Detroit Red Wings in return for a small but effective centre who would play on two Stanley Cup–winning teams for the Habs (in 1946 and 1953). He recorded 265 points for Montreal before he retired. Who was he?
Hint: He was a very good coach with the Chicago Blackhawks in the 1960s and 1970s.

5) Prior to the start of the 1947–48 season, the Canadiens made a rather unpopular deal when they sent this centre to the New York Rangers, along with defenceman Frank Eddolls, in return for Hal Laycoe, Joe Bell and George Robertson. The New York–bound centre was a two-time Stanley Cup winner in Montreal (1944 and 1946) and went on to win the Hart Trophy for the 1947–48 season. Who was he?

6) This big left winger (six foot three and 192 pounds) from Winnipeg, Manitoba, first joined the Canadiens in 1957–58 and promptly won three Stanley Cups with the team. Once seen as a rising star, he was dealt to Chicago in June of 1960 along with the rights to Reggie Fleming, and was on the Blackhawks' Stanley Cup–winning team of 1961. Who was he?

7) When Montreal coach Toe Blake got fed up with the antics of goalie Jacques Plante, the Habs dealt the flakey netminder to the New York Rangers, along with Don Marshall and Phil Goyette, in exchange for three players in June of 1963. Who did the Canadiens get back in return?

Doug Jarvis (#21) won the Stanley Cup in each of his first four years in the NHL.

8) In June of 1964 the Canadiens sent two players they had drafted (Guy Allen and Paul Reid) to the Boston Bruins in return for this goalie who would go on to win six Stanley Cups

Mario Tremblay (#14) coached the Canadiens between 1995 and 1997.

and post a 258–57–74 regular-season record for the Habs. Who did Montreal acquire in the deal?

9) The Canadiens acquired this tough, rugged blueliner from Springfield of the American Hockey League in June of 1963 in a trade that involved mostly minor-league players. The big blueliner (six foot two, 183 pounds) joined the Habs full time for the 1964–65 season and went on to play on four Stanley Cup teams in Montreal. He also played for Minnesota, Detroit, St. Louis and Philadelphia. Who was he?

10) Defenceman and sometime right winger Bryan "Bugsy" Watson had two different stints with the Canadiens, and they traded him away each time. The second deal (completed on June 28, 1968) involving Watson netted the Habs a first-round draft choice in 1972 courtesy of the Oakland Seals. Who did the Canadiens select with the draft pick?

11) With the eighth choice overall in the 1972 Amateur Draft, the Canadiens selected centre Dave Gardner, who had just completed a great junior career with the Toronto Marlboros. Although Gardner did not stay long in Montreal (a total of 36 games), he was used to acquire another first-round pick from St. Louis. The pick the Habs used to select Gardner had been obtained from Minnesota for two players in June of 1968. Can you name both players?

12) Bobby Rousseau had been a very good player for the Canadiens (including two 30-goal seasons and four Stanley Cup victories), but when the Habs missed the playoffs in 1970, changes were made and he was dealt to the Minnesota North Stars. Who did Montreal receive in return?
Hint: He was a former Canadien player who had won the Cup with Montreal in 1965, 1966 and 1968.

13) When Frank Mahovlich was traded to Detroit, he did very well, scoring 49 goals in 1968–69. However, the Detroit club was in disarray just

two years later and they sent the Big M to Montreal for three players. It was a good deal for both teams, and Mahovlich won two Stanley Cups as a Hab. Which three players were sent to the Motor City?

14) Although defenceman Bob Murdoch had helped the Canadiens win two Stanley Cups (1971 and 1973), there was no room for him on the roster after the 1972–73 season. The Habs packaged him, along with the rights to Randy Rota, to the Los Angeles Kings in return for a first-round draft choice in 1974. Who did Montreal select with that pick?
Hint: He would coach the Canadiens in the 1990s.

15) Goaltender Michel "Bunny" Larocque was a very good backup goalie during the Canadiens' glory days of the 1970s, sharing the Vezina Trophy three times with Ken Dryden. However, when Dryden retired, Larocque was never seen as the number one netminder. Eventually he was traded to Toronto for a defenceman who had been drafted third overall in 1977. Who did the Habs get in the March 10, 1981, swap?

16) When Canadiens defenceman Rod Langway demanded a trade (citing tax reasons), the team had no choice but to accommodate his wishes. Langway was sent to the Washington Capitals along with Brian Engblom,

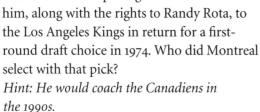

Ryan Walter came to the Canadiens in a trade with the Washington Capitals.

Doug Jarvis and Craig Laughlin. Which players did the Canadiens receive in return? *Hint: Both players helped Montreal win the Stanley Cup in 1986.*

17) Montreal general manager Serge Savard made an excellent deal when he acquired Bobby Smith from the Minnesota North Stars on October 28, 1983. Smith was a major contributor to the Montreal Stanley Cup win in 1986. Who did the North Stars get from the Canadiens?

18) By the time the Canadiens decided to trade defenceman Robert Picard, he was no longer considered a potential star in the making. The Habs found a willing taker in the Winnipeg Jets on November 4, 1983, but were only able to secure a 1984 third-round draft choice in return (although it worked out very well for the Canadiens in the long run). Who did the Habs select with their choice?

19) A June 9, 1981, deal saw the Canadiens send goalie Rick Wamsley, along with three draft

choices, to the St. Louis Blues in exchange for a first-round draft choice and a second-round pick in the 1984 Entry Draft. Who did the Habs take with the two choices?

20) The Canadiens (especially coach Pat Burns) grew tired of Claude Lemieux, and even though he had been a large part of the Stanley Cup win in 1986, they traded him to New Jersey on September 4, 1990. Who did the Canadiens get in return?
Hint: This player was a former first-round draft choice of the Hartford Whalers in 1983.

21) General manager Serge Savard made another major swap in September of 1991, when he was able to acquire Kirk Muller from the New Jersey Devils (along with goaltender Roland Melanson). Which two players did Savard send to the Devils to complete the swap?

22) Serge Savard made another big deal when he sent Shayne Corson, Brent Gilchrist and Vladimir Vujtek to the Edmonton Oilers on August 27, 1992, to obtain a Montreal native who would lead the Habs in points during the 1992–93 season. He also helped the Habs win the Stanley Cup in 1993, when he had 20 points in the playoffs. Who was he?

23) The Canadiens were left with no choice but to trade one of the best players in team history when Patrick Roy made it clear to team president Ronald Corey that he could not get along with coach Mario Tremblay and had played his last game as a Hab. On December 6, 1995, the team sent Roy and Mike Keane to Colorado in exchange for three players. Who did they get in return?

24) A March 1, 2000, deal saw Montreal unload enigmatic defenceman Vladimir Malakhov to the New Jersey Devils. In return the Canadiens got a big blueliner (six foot four, 225 pounds) who scored 15 goals in 2003–04 and 26 goals in 2006–07. Who is he?

25) Montreal general manager Bob Gainey was fortunate to find a team that was interested in taking on the large contract of slumping netminder Jose Theodore on March 8, 2006. The Colorado Avalanche agreed to a swap of goalies. Who did the Canadiens get in return?

26) When Montreal traded goalie Jeff Hackett to the San Jose Sharks on January 23, 2003, they

Goaltender Patrick Roy (#33) was a rookie in 1986 when he took the Canadiens to a Stanley Cup championship.

received a forward who had been drafted eighth overall by the New York Rangers in 1993. He once scored 24 goals (in 1996–97) for the Rangers, but he never scored more than eight in one season with Montreal. Who was he?

27) Acquired in a trade with Los Angeles in 2004, this netminder helped take the Canadiens to the playoffs in 2006 with an 18–11–4 record in the 2005–06 regular season. He recorded seven shutouts and also led the NHL in save percentage (at .929). Who is he?

Montreal forwards Claude Lemieux (#32) and Bobby Smith (#15) storm the Maple Leaf net.

28) Originally signed as a free agent out of Bowling Green by Toronto in 1997, this winger also went on to play for Tampa Bay and Phoenix before the Habs sent a fourth-round draft choice to the Coyotes on July 12, 2006, for his rights. He scored 20 or more goals twice in his career, but would only score 11 with the Habs in 2006–07. Name him.

REMEMBER HIM?

1) This native of Montreal was one the best defenceman of his era, and he joined the Canadiens after a trade with Hamilton for Harry Mummery and Amos Arbour on November 26, 1921. He helped Montreal win the Stanley Cup in 1924 and also shared in a championship with the Ottawa Senators on two other occasions (1920 and 1921). He finished his career with Boston. Who was this Hall of Fame blueliner?

2) A native of Quebec, this centre joined the Canadiens in 1925–26 and was on two (1930 and 1931) Stanley Cup winners with the Habs. He recorded 241 points in 526 career games — all played for the Canadiens. His best season in Montreal came in 1929–30, when he scored 24 and totalled 33 points. Who was he?

3) Born in Montreal, Quebec, this defenceman played 538 games for the Canadiens before he finished his career by playing in four contests for the Boston Bruins in 1936–37. The Hall of Fame blueliner was on three Stanley Cup–winning teams (1924, 1930 and 1931) for the Habs and recorded 141 points (including 63 goals). His brother Georges also played for the Canadiens over many of the same years. Who was he?

4) Signed as a free agent by the Canadiens in October of 1940, this centre from Ottawa, Ontario, would only play in 119 games for the Habs before he was traded along with Jimmy Peters to Boston for Joe Carveth. While he was with the Canadiens, this player was named rookie of the year in 1940–41, when he had 18 goals and 34 points in 48 games. Who was he?

5) Born in Montreal on September 11, 1920, this robust defenceman (six foot two, 205 pounds) joined the Canadiens in 1941–42. He would go on to play on four Stanley Cup teams

Vince Damphousse (#25) had a very good playoff for the Canadiens in 1993.

(1944, 1946, 1953, 1956) with the Habs before his Hall of Fame career was over. Besides being named team captain, this blueliner was an NHL All-Star four times (three on the first team) and finished with 193 points in 785 career games — all with Montreal. Can you name him?
Hint: His son also played for the Canadiens in the 1970s.

6) This right winger from Shawinigan, Quebec, joined the Canadiens in 1956–57 and was on a Stanley Cup–winning team in each of the first four years of his career. He scored 16 times in 1957–58 for the Habs, his career-best total for one season. Early in the 1960–61 season he was dealt to Boston for Jean-Guy Gendron. He also played for Detroit and Minnesota before he retired. Who was he?

7) This defenceman from Regina, Saskatchewan, had his best season for the Canadiens in 1958–59, when he scored a career high in assists (24) and points (28), and he was on the Montreal club that won five straight Stanley Cups between 1956 and 1960. He was dealt to Chicago in the summer of 1961 and scored eight goals for the Blackhawks in 1961–62. Name him.

8) This blueliner from Verdun, Quebec, first played for the Habs in 1950–51, when he appeared in three contests. He would play on four Stanley Cup–winning teams with Montreal and had his best year in 1957–58, when he recorded 23 points. He was dealt to Chicago in the summer of 1958 and was with the Blackhawks when they took the Cup in 1961. Who was he?

9) Born on November 6, 1934, this native of Magog, Quebec, joined the Montreal Canadiens in 1957–58 when he played in just one regular-season game and seven playoff games. The large blueliner won three Stanley Cups with Montreal, but was dealt to the New York Rangers in June of 1961 for John Hanna. He also played for Detroit and Boston. Who was he?

Defenceman Butch Bouchard (wearing the "C" on his sweater) was elected to the Hockey Hall of Fame.

10) One of the first players to make the NHL out of the U.S. college system *and* one of the first to wear a helmet, this playmaking centre started his career with Montreal in 1961–62. He was on the Habs' Stanley Cup team of 1965 but was dealt to the New York Rangers in 1966. He had his best NHL seasons with St. Louis and Detroit. Who was he?

11) Acquired by the Habs in the trade that saw the great Doug Harvey go to the New York Rangers in 1961, this defenceman from Guelph, Ontario, led the NHL in penalty minutes in 1961–62 with 167. His career came to an end the following season when he suffered a severe neck injury. Who was he?

12) A June 1960 deal saw the Canadiens send Stan Smrke to the Maple Leafs in exchange for a defenceman from Sydney, Nova Scotia, who would only play for Montreal during the 1961–62 season (one goal and eight points in 61 games played). He was then sent to the Chicago Blackhawks and also played for New York and Pittsburgh before his playing days were over. Who was he?
Hint: He coached the Canadiens to the Stanley Cup in 1971.

13) One of the NHL's best two-way players when he was with Montreal between 1960 and 1969, this left winger from Montmorency, Quebec, played his entire 509-game career as a Hab. He was on three Stanley Cup teams with the Canadiens and scored 168 goals and totalled 330 points. He went on to have a great career as a broadcaster. Who is he?

14) This tough but low-scoring defenceman joined the Canadiens for the 1962–63 season when he played in 14 contests. He was a full-time Hab in 1963–64 and recorded 17 points in 70 games played. He would win five Stanley Cups (1964, 1965, 1968, 1969 and 1971) with the Canadiens, but didn't want to stay in Montreal after Scotty Bowman took over as coach. He was dealt to the Los Angeles Kings in August of 1972 and would also play for Detroit, St. Louis and Colorado. Can you name him?

15) One of the most useful and versatile players ever to wear the Canadiens uniform, this native of Toronto, Ontario, first played for the Habs between 1963 and 1967 (playing on two Stanley Cup teams). The defenceman/right winger was claimed by the St. Louis Blues in the 1967 Expansion Draft but was re-acquired by Montreal in a 1972 trade. He won three more Cups in 1973, 1976 and 1977 before playing one more season back in St. Louis. Who was he? *Hint: He coached Buffalo, Hartford and St. Louis, each for only one season.*

16) On November 29, 1977, the Canadiens acquired this native of Tashereau, Quebec, from the Pittsburgh Penguins in exchange for Peter Mahovlich and Peter Lee. He won two Stanley Cups with the Habs (1978 and 1979) and scored 50 goals in 1979–80. He would also play for Hartford and the New York Rangers before he retired. Can you name this player who scored 395 career goals?

17) Drafted fifth overall by the Canadiens in 1974, this big right winger (six foot two, 200 pounds) from Winnipeg, Manitoba, played only one season (23 games in 1978–79, scoring a goal and assisting on three others) for the Habs and got his name on the Stanley Cup. His lone playoff goal in the '79 post-season was an overtime winner against Toronto. He also played for Edmonton and the New York Rangers. Who was he?

18) This right winger from Calgary, Alberta, was drafted by Montreal in 1975 (52nd overall) and he was with the Canadiens when they won the Stanley Cup in 1979. He was dealt to Pittsburgh in the trade that landed the Canadiens goaltender Denis Heron but he was moved to Edmonton, where he once scored five goals in one game. He also won two more Cups as an Oiler (in 1984 and 1985). Name him.

19) This goaltender from Ste-Foy, Quebec, first made his mark in the 1984 playoffs when he

Defenceman Dollard St. Laurent won three Stanley Cups with Montreal.

won nine games and got the Habs past the Boston Bruins and the Quebec Nordiques before losing to the New York Islanders. He won 26 games in 1984–85, but only got into 18 games in 1985–86. He was soon dealt to the Winnipeg Jets, where he played parts of two seasons. Name him.

20) This right winger from Timra, Sweden, joined the Canadiens for the 1985–86 season, when he scored 32 goals. He scored two goals and

added three assists in the '86 post-season, which saw the Habs win the Stanley Cup. He scored 25 goals over the next two seasons in Montreal but was then gone from the NHL. Can you name him?

21) The Canadiens selected this left winger from Drummondville, Quebec, 81st overall in 1990, and he joined the team for two games in 1990–91. He scored 21 times in just 39 games the following season and then had 20 in 1992–93. The '93 post-season saw him score six goals and six assists as the Canadiens took the Stanley Cup. A 19-goal season the next year was followed by a trade to Philadelphia, where he did not score a single goal in 22 games as a Flyer. Who was he?
Hint: His brother was a Hall of Fame player with Detroit, Los Angeles and New York.

Gilles Tremblay (#21) was a very good two-way player for the Canadiens.

22) This smallish (five foot seven, 160 pounds) left winger first played for the Canadiens in 1982–83 and quickly established himself as one the better players in the NHL. In his eight seasons in Montreal he never scored fewer than 21 goals, with a career-high 43 in 1985–86. He had 19 points in 20 playoff games in the '86 post-season, when the Habs won the Stanley Cup. He finished with 614 points as a Canadien and played one year for the Boston Bruins in 1994–95. Who was he?
Hint: He won the Lady Byng Trophy in 1988.

23) Drafted second overall by Minnesota in 1982, this right winger joined the Canadiens after a trade for the start of the 1992–93 season — a year that saw him score 40 goals and total 88 points. He added 15 points in 18 playoff games as the Habs won the Stanley Cup, and he scored 33 times in 1993–94. He was dealt to Tampa Bay in 1995 and also played for Anaheim and Washington before his career was over. Who was he?

24) This big left winger from Vermont was selected 33rd overall by the Canadiens in 1987 and is best remembered in Montreal for scoring consecutive overtime goals against the Los Angeles Kings in the 1993 Stanley Cup finals. He never scored more than 19 goals in a season for the Habs, but a trade to Philadelphia saw him score 51, 50 and 51 for the Flyers between 1995 and 1998. Who was he?

25) The Canadiens were very excited when they acquired this centre from the New York

Islanders in April of 1995 since the native of Rouyn, Quebec, was coming home. Originally drafted first overall by the Buffalo Sabres in 1987, the smooth playmaker usually recorded between 80 and 100 points a season. Things never really worked out in Montreal for this player, despite the fact that he had a 96-point season in 1995–96 and was named team captain. He was traded to the St. Louis Blues in October of 1996. Who is he?

26) Selected 13th overall by Montreal in 2000 after playing U.S. college hockey, this six-foot, three-inch, 211-pound defenceman would only play in 32 games for the Canadiens (recording one goal and one assist) before he was lost to Columbus on waivers in 2005. Who was he?

27) Although he was a native of Montreal and was drafted 45th overall by the Canadiens, centre Mike Ribeiro was never a popular figure in the Habs' dressing room. He did score 20 goals for Montreal in 2003–04 and 16 the next year, but he was traded to the Dallas Stars. Who did Montreal receive in return?

28) When Guy Carbonneau took over as coach of the Canadiens for the 2006–07 season, this defenceman fell out of favour with him. The rugged blueliner was a Hab his entire career, starting in 1994–95, and had his best point total in Montreal during the 2005–06 season with 34 (7 goals, 27 assists). He was dealt to San Jose late in the 2006–07 season for

another defenceman and a first-round draft choice. Who was the defenceman in question, and who did the Sharks sent to Montreal?

DID YOU KNOW?

1) Which legendary Montreal player is honoured in a story quoted on the back of the Canadian five-dollar bill?
a) Howie Morenz b) Maurice Richard
c) Jean Beliveau

2) This defenceman first joined the Canadiens for the 1954–55 season and would be on seven Stanley Cup teams in Montreal before he was claimed by Minnesota in the 1967 Expansion Draft. He played in the finals three times with the St. Louis Blues and also played briefly for Detroit and Buffalo. He later coached the Blues and the New York Rangers. Can you name him?

3) One of the best offensive defencemen of his time and a two-time NHL All-Star, this native

Montreal defencemen Jacques Laperriere (#2) and J. C. Tremblay (#3) defend against Toronto's Frank Mahovlich.

of Bagotville, Quebec, was very upset when he was not given the Conn Smythe Trophy after the Canadiens won the Stanley Cup in 1966 (it was awarded to Detroit's Roger Crozier instead). A good puckhandler (306 career assists for the Canadiens), this blueliner did not play a rugged game but was with the Habs for five Stanley Cups before he went to the World Hockey Association. His sweater number 3 was retired by the Quebec Nordiques. Who was he?

4) For the first time in history, the NHL All-Star Game was played during the middle of the season when the Canadiens faced a team of league All-Stars at the Forum on January 18, 1967. The Habs won the game 3–0, and two netminders shared the very unusual All-Star game shutout. Who were the two goalies, and which Canadien was named the most valuable player of the game?

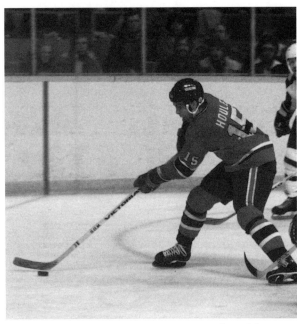

Rejean Houle won five Stanley Cups as a member of the Canadiens.

5) He was written off as a "Junior B goaltender" when he faced the Maple Leafs in the 1967 Stanley Cup finals, but this netminder helped the Habs to two Stanley Cups (1968 and 1969) and shared a Vezina Trophy with Gump Worsley (in '68). He asked for a trade once Ken Dryden took over in goal for Montreal, and he was sent to the Los Angeles Kings. Who was he?

6) In the 1969 Amateur Draft, the Canadiens had one last opportunity to select two top players from the province of Quebec before any other team selected. With the first- and second-overall picks, the Habs took two wingers. Both players were with the Canadiens when they won the Stanley Cup in 1971 and 1973. Name both of them.
Hint: Both would jump to the World Hockey Association.

Goaltender Charlie Hodge was on four Stanley Cup–winning teams with Montreal.

7) Six members of the 1971–72 Canadiens were selected to play for Team Canada in the historic Summit Series of 1972. Name all six who helped Canada defeat the Soviet Union in the eight-game series.

8) This Hall of Fame netminder began his NHL career with the Canadiens during the 1968–69 season and he recorded his first shutout that

Youngster Chris Higgins scored 22 times for Montreal in 2006–07.

same year, when the Habs beat Philadelphia 1–0. He earned another against Boston at the Forum on December 21, 1968, when he made 41 saves in a scoreless tie. Beginning in 1969–70,

he played the rest of his career with Chicago, recording a total of 76 shutouts. Who was he?

9) When Toe Blake decided to retire immediately after the Canadiens won the Stanley Cup in 1968, he was replaced by a stocky 30-year-old who really was not that interested in coaching. He posted a 172–82–51 career mark overall and won the Cup with Montreal in 1969. Who was he?

10) Drafted fourth overall by the Canadiens in 1972, this left winger from Toronto turned out to be one of the best goal scorers in Montreal history. He had a career-best 60 goals in 1976–77 and scored 30 or more nine times for the Habs. He was elected to the Hall of Fame. Who was he?

11) Guy Lafleur scored 518 career goals for the Canadiens, but he never had a five-goal night. How many times did he score four goals in one game?

12) On May 22, 1986, the Canadiens became the first team to record 100 wins in the Stanley Cup finals when they beat the Calgary Flames 1–0 at the Forum. Which goaltender earned his first playoff shutout in that same game?

13) On May 19, 1989, this Habs defenceman became the first player to appear in 200 career playoff games when Montreal beat Calgary 4–3 in overtime at the Forum. Who was this blueliner?

14) The Canadiens' 1–0 loss to the Pittsburgh Penguins on December 1, 1997, marked the 5,000th game in team history. Of those 5,000 contests, how many did the Habs win?
a) 1,595 b) 2,020 c) 2,450 d) 2,625

15) Though the team has enjoyed having some of the best seasons in the history of the NHL, only two coaches of the Montreal Canadiens have ever won the Jack Adams Award. Can you name both?

16) True or false: The Canadiens never had fewer than 100 points in any of Scotty Bowman's eight seasons behind the bench.

Yvan Cournoyer (#12) and John Ferguson (#22) of the Canadiens try to get one past Johnny Bower of the Maple Leafs.

17) The night of January 12, 1985, saw the Canadiens announce their 75th anniversary team, consisting of a coach, a goalie, two defencemen and three forwards. Can you name all those who were selected?

18) The last NHL All-Star Game played at the Montreal Forum was on February 6, 1993, and saw the Wales Conference score a 16–6 win over the Campbell Conference. Which two Montreal players were on the winning side in the contest?

19) When the Montreal Canadiens won the Stanley Cup in 1993, they won a remarkable 10 consecutive games in overtime (after losing their first extra-session game in the '93 playoffs to the Quebec Nordiques). Eric Desjardins and John LeClair scored overtime winners in the Stanley Cup finals against Los Angeles. Who scored the other OT winning goals, and which goaltender played in all the games?
Hint: There are five different scorers to be named.

20) During the 1995–96 season, Canadien goaltender Jocelyn Thibault paid tribute to a legendary Montreal netminder by having that player's picture painted on his mask by artist Michel Lefebvre. Which netminder did Thibault honour?
a) Jacques Plante b) Bill Durnan
c) Georges Vezina

21) This native of Bonavista, Newfoundland, led all NHL rookies in assists (38) and points (63) with the Canadiens in 2003–04 but lost out on the Calder Trophy to Boston netminder Andrew Raycroft. The right winger scored 30 goals in 2005–06 and again in 2006–07. Who is he?

22) Acquired in a deal with the New York Rangers in March of 2004 (for Jozef Balej and a draft choice), this very talented right winger led the Habs in points during the 2005–06 season with 65 in 69 games played (23 goals, 42 assists). Who is he?

23) Sweater number 18 was retired by the Canadiens during a ceremony in the 2006–07 season in honour of defenceman Serge Savard. The Montreal blueliner is a member of the Hall of Fame and one of the last players to wear the number for the Canadiens was also elected to the hallowed Hall. Who was he?

24) During the 2006–07 season, the Montreal Canadiens retired sweater number 29 in honour of goaltending great Ken Dryden. Who was the last Montreal player to wear that number on his jersey?

25) Drafted 21st overall by Montreal in 1993, this centre from Turku, Finland, was named captain of the Canadiens in 1999. He has scored 20 or more goals three times as a Hab and was named winner of the Masterton Trophy in 2002. Who is he?

26) One of the few Swiss-born players to suit up for an NHL team, this defenceman was drafted 262nd overall by the Habs in 2004. He joined the Habs in 2005–06, playing in 48 games and recording 11 points. He had a good season in 2006–07, when he had 36 points for Montreal. Who is he?

27) A rookie with Montreal in 2005–06 season, this native of Smithtown, New York, scored 23 times for the Canadiens and also contributed three short-handed tallies. He was drafted 14th overall by Montreal in 2002 after a career at Yale University, and scored 22 goals in 2006–07. Who is he?

28) Selected eighth overall by Boston in 1997, this smallish (five-feet, eight-inch) right winger scored 20 or more goals four times for the Bruins and had 23 during the 2005–06 season, which he split between Boston and Edmonton. The Canadiens signed him to a lucrative contract as free agent on July 12, 2006, but they ended up putting him on waivers at one point during the 2006–07 season — a year that saw him score just nine goals. Who is he?

Saku Koivu was selected 21st overall by Montreal in 1993.

NEW YORK RANGERS

Goaltender Lorne "Gump" Worsley makes a save on Toronto's Bob Nevin.

MEMORABLE GAMES

1) The New York Rangers joined the NHL at the start of the 1926–27 season. Where did they play their first game (on November 16, 1926), and who provided the opposition?

2) By the end of their second season (1927–28), the Rangers had made it to the Stanley Cup finals, meeting the Montreal Maroons for the championship. Montreal won the first game 2–0, and the second game of the series, played on April 7, saw Ranger netminder Lorne Chabot suffer an eye injury. Who filled in for Chabot, and what was the final result?

3) The Rangers won their first-ever Stanley Cup on the night of April 14, 1928, when they beat the Maroons 2–1 in Montreal in the fifth and final game of the series. One player scored both Ranger goals to secure the championship. Who was he?
Hint: He won the Lady Byng Trophy a total of seven times during his career.

4) The Rangers were back in the Stanley Cup finals in 1929, but they lost the best-of-three series 2–0. The last game was played on March 29, 1929, in New York, and the Rangers went down to a 2–1 defeat. Who was the opposition, and why was the matchup an NHL first?

5) The Rangers advanced to the Stanley Cup finals once again in 1932 after beating the Montreal Canadiens three games to one in their best-of-five first-round playoff series. The key contest in the series was the second game in Montreal, which the New York club won 4–3 after 59:32 of overtime. Who scored the winning goal?

6) The Rangers were back in the Stanley Cup finals in 1933 and were able to open the series at home on April 4 against the favoured Toronto Maple Leafs. Although the rest of the series had to be played in Toronto (due to the circus taking over Madison Square Garden), the Rangers did open the series with a victory on home ice. What was the final score of the only game played in New York?

7) The night of April 13, 1933, saw the Rangers win their second Stanley Cup when they beat Toronto 1–0 in overtime in the fourth game of the series, played at Maple Leaf Gardens. Who scored the winning goal?

8) On March 25, 1937, the Rangers defeated the Toronto Maple Leafs 2–1 on home ice to

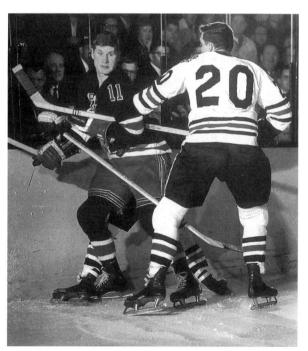

Vic Hadfield (#11) was captain of the Rangers from 1971 to 1974.

earn a spot in the Stanley Cup semi-finals. The winning goal allowed the Rangers to take the quarter-final series in two straight games. Who scored the winner for the Rangers after 13:05 of extra play?
Hint: This player would star for the Maple Leafs a few years later.

9) April 1 and 3, 1937, saw this Ranger netminder record back-to-back shutouts during a best-of-three semi-final versus the Montreal Maroons to earn a spot in the Stanley Cup finals. The Rangers won the games by scores of 1–0 and 4–0. Who was the Ranger netminder who posted the shutouts?

10) The Rangers opened the 1937 Stanley Cup finals with a 5–1 home-ice win against the

Goaltender Henrik Lundqvist posted a 37-22-8 record in 2006–07 for New York.

Detroit Red Wings, but then proceeded to lose three of the next four games (all played in Detroit). The Red Wings clinched the Cup with consecutive shutouts, the latter coming on April 15, when this rookie netminder became the first goalie to post two shutouts in the finals. Can you name this Detroit goalie?

11) March 22, 24, and 27, 1938, saw the Rangers meet their rivals the New York Americans in the playoffs for the first time. The best-of-three series was won 2–1 by the Americans on the strength of an overtime goal in the third game. Who scored the series-winner for the Americans?

12) New York and Boston played a best-of-seven semi-final in the 1939 playoffs and the Rangers

Rod Gilbert (#7) is a member of the Hockey Hall of Fame.

were done in by three overtime losses to the Bruins. The final OT loss came on April 2, when the Bruins won 2–1 to take the series four games to three. The player who scored the winner that night also scored the other two overtime winners for Boston in the series. Who was he?

Mark Messier (#11) was acquired by the Rangers in a trade with the Edmonton Oilers.

13) The Rangers regained the Stanley Cup by beating the Toronto Maple Leafs in six games in the 1940 finals. Three of the Ranger victories came in overtime, including the final game of the series, played at Maple Leaf Gardens on April 13. Who scored the Cup winner for the Rangers after 2:07 of extra play?

14) The 1950 Stanley Cup final was a classic seven-game series that the Rangers lost in overtime of the last game. They did, however, win two extra-time sessions in the series against Detroit. One Ranger scored both of these overtime winners, on the nights of April 18 and 20. Who was he?

15) In 1971, the Rangers beat Toronto in six games in the first round of the playoff series. New York then played Chicago in the semi-final and lost a tough series in seven games. The seventh game was made necessary when this Ranger scored after 41:29 of overtime of the sixth game on April 29, giving his team a 3–2 victory. Who was he?

16) This player became the first New York Ranger to score 50 goals in a season when he tallied twice on April 2, 1972, in a 6–5 loss to the Montreal Canadiens at Madison Square Garden. Who was this high-scoring Ranger, and which Montreal netminder allowed the goal?

17) New York made it back to the Stanley Cup finals in 1972 (their first trip since 1950) by knocking off Montreal (the defending champions) in six games during the first round, then sweeping their next opponent in four straight games. Which team did New York sweep?

18) The Rangers lost a very bitter seven-game semi-final to Philadelphia in the 1974 semi-finals. In the fourth game, played on April 28, they tied the series at two games apiece with a home-ice victory at MSG. Who scored the OT winner after 4:20 of extra play to give the Rangers a new lease on life in the series?

19) The Rangers were shocked to be eliminated by the New York Islanders when they played at home on April 11, 1975, during the third and

final frame of a best-of-three series. The Islanders scored after just 11 seconds of overtime to knock the Rangers out of the post-season with a 4–3 victory. Who scored the goal?

20) Before they were beaten in five games by the Montreal Canadiens in the 1979 Stanley Cup finals, the upstart Rangers beat Los Angeles, Philadelphia and the Islanders. After beating L.A. 7–1 at the Garden in the first game of their preliminary-round series, they travelled across country, eliminating the Kings 2–1 in overtime on April 12. Who scored the game- and series-winner for New York?

21) The 1984 Patrick Division semi-final between the Rangers and the Islanders was a classic

Brian Leetch (#2) was selected ninth overall in 1986 by the Rangers.

five-game series that ended on an overtime goal in the fifth and deciding game played on April 10. Who was the unlikely goal scorer for the Islanders, and which Ranger netminder allowed the marker that gave the Islanders a 3–2 victory?

22) The Rangers were not expected to go very far in the 1986 playoffs, but they knocked off Philadelphia in the first round and then took on the Washington Capitals in the Patrick Division final. The Rangers took the series in six games, winning two of the contests in overtime. The first OT win came on April 17 in Washington, while the other occurred at home on April 23. Which players scored the winning goals?

23) May 25, 1994, saw one the greatest performances in Rangers history when, with his team facing elimination at the hands of the New Jersey Devils, this player scored three goals. The hat trick helped the Rangers win the contest 4–2 and kept their hopes alive for a berth in the Stanley Cup finals. Who had guaranteed that the Rangers would win this game played in New Jersey, and who scored the hat trick?

24) In the seventh game of that 1994 Eastern Conference final series against New Jersey, played on May 27, the Rangers were again nearly eliminated by the Devils in the seventh game. The Devils tied the contest 1–1 in the last minute of play to force the contest into overtime. It took 24:24 of extra play to decide matters, but the Rangers pulled out a victory. Who scored the overtime goal?
Hint: It was his second overtime winner of the series against New Jersey.

25) On June 14, 1994, when the Rangers finally won the Stanley Cup for the first time since 1940, they did so at Madison Square Garden, beating Vancouver 3–2 in the seventh game of the series. Which players scored the Ranger goals, and which one was the game winner?

26) Ranger winger Jaromir Jagr enjoyed the third 50-goal season of his career in 2005–06. He scored number 50 on March 24, 2006, when the Rangers beat the Florida Panthers 3–2. Which goaltender allowed the milestone goal?

27) In 2005–06, the NHL instituted a shootout as a way of settling regular-season games still tied after a five-minute overtime period. The longest shootout of the 2005–06 season took place between the Rangers and Washington Capitals at Madison Square Garden on November 26, 2005. It ended when this New York defenceman scored a spectacular goal by putting his stick between his legs and then flipping a shot over the shoulder of Capital goalie Olaf Kolzig. Who scored the goal?

28) On October 5, 2006, during the season home opener, this Ranger scored two goals against the Washington Capitals to pace his team to a 5–2 win. In the process, he scored the 600th marker of his career. He joined the Rangers as a free agent after winning three Stanley Cups with Detroit. Who is he?

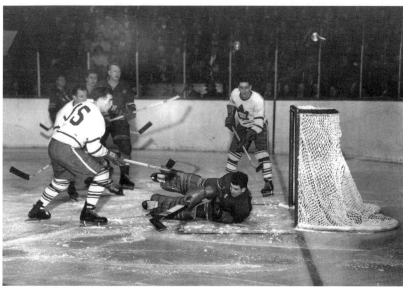

Goaltender Chuck Rayner stops Toronto's Tod Sloan in close.

RECORDS AND AWARDS

1) On November 11, 1930, the Rangers took part in the first-ever NHL game played in the city of Philadelphia, against the Quakers (formerly the Pittsburgh Pirates). What was the result of the contest?

2) This Ranger left winger played in his 500th consecutive game for the team on February 23, 1937, when the Rangers lost 2–1 to the Maple Leafs. The two-time Stanley Cup winner (1928 and 1933) appeared in 508 career games with New York between his debut in 1926 and his retirement in 1937, all of them played consecutively. Who was this early iron man?

3) Acquired in a cash deal with Boston in 1943, this centre would lead the Rangers in goals, assists and points for two consecutive seasons (1944–45 and 1945–46). His best year was in 1944–45, when he had 24 goals and 30 assists

for New York, but he was gone from the NHL by the end of the 1946–47 season. Who was he? *Hint: His son was a Ranger defenceman between 1969–70 and 1971–72.*

4) One of the few goaltenders to win the Hart Trophy as the NHL's best player, this New York netminder won the coveted award for his performance during the 1949–50 season when he won 28 games (although he lost 30)with six shutouts and a 2.62 goals-against average. He then took the Rangers to the Stanley Cup finals. Who was he?

5) Nicknamed "The Eel" this native of Quebec City was named rookie of the year for his performance in 1953–54, when he scored 24 goals in 66 games. He scored 20 or more goals another eight times as a Ranger (notching a career-best 37 in 1962–63) before he was dealt to Chicago. Who was he?

6) This outstanding right winger won the Hart Trophy as the NHL's most valuable player in 1958–59 despite the fact the Rangers missed the playoffs that year. He had 40 goals and 48 assists for 88 points in the 70-game regular season. Who was he?

7) This six-foot, one-inch, 195-pound defenceman from Guelph, Ontario, joined the Rangers for 27 games in the 1954–55 season. He became a regular the following year and led the NHL in

penalty minutes with 202, repeating the feat in 1957–58 with 152. He never recorded fewer than 100 minutes in any of his nine NHL seasons, seven of which were spent in New York. A 1961 trade sent him to Montreal. Can you name him?

8) On March 22, 1964, this former Ranger set a league mark (since surpassed) by playing in his 630th consecutive game. He played his last game on that night as a Boston Bruin but had played eight full years (1955–56 to 1962–63) as a Ranger without missing a single game — a team-record 560 straight appearances. Who was this very durable performer?

9) A January 21, 1967, contest between New York and Boston saw this Ranger become the first player in team history to play in 1,000 career games. Which player hit the milestone in the Rangers' 6–2 loss to the Bruins?

10) The Rangers set a team record for goals in one game when they trounced the California Seals

Camille Henry scored 24 goals as a rookie in 1953–54 for the Rangers.

12–1 on November 21, 1971, at Madison Square Garden. One Ranger player set a club record by scoring two goals in eight seconds. Who was he?

11) On February 18, 1972, during a 2–2 tie against the California Seals, this longtime Ranger star became the first player in team history to record 100 points in one season. Who was he?

Defenceman Lou Fontinato (left) is about to move in on Toronto's Gerry James in front of New York netminder Gump Worsley.

12) The holder of many team records, this popular Ranger became the first player in team history to record his 1,000th point in a New York uniform. He hit the milestone on February 19, 1977, when the Rangers lost 5–2 to the New York Islanders. Who was he?

13) An NHL first-team All-Star on five occasions, this blueliner holds the team record for most goals in one season by a defenceman (25 in 1974–75). Who was he?

14) This New York rookie tied an NHL record when he scored five goals in one game against the Minnesota North Stars on October 12, 1976. He would finish the season with 32 goals and then go on to score 27 the following year. Who was he?

15) This Ranger set an NHL record by recording six assists in one playoff game during a 7–3 New York win over the Philadelphia Flyers on April 8, 1982. Can you name him?

16) A former member of the 1980 U.S. Olympic team that won the gold medal at Lake Placid, this centre scored five goals in one game when the Rangers beat the Hartford Whalers 11–3 on February 23, 1983. Who had the big night?

17) The Rangers selected this goaltender 72nd overall in 1981 and the native of Detroit, Michigan, was the first New York netminder to win the Vezina Trophy under the new criteria established in 1982. He won the award for his performance in the 1985–86 season when he led the league with 31 wins, also earning a spot on the NHL's first All-Star team that season. Who was he?

18) How many New York Ranger defencemen have won the Norris Trophy since its inception in 1954?
a) 2 b) 3 c) 4

19) How many times have the Rangers won the Presidents' Trophy (first awarded in 1986) for

finishing with the best record in the NHL?
a) 2 b) 3 c) 4

20) Acquired in a trade with Edmonton, this hard-working centre scored his 50th goal of the season on March 23, 1994, when the Rangers beat the Oilers 5–3. He would finish the season with 52 and was a big part of the New York's Stanley Cup win in 1994. Who was he, and which former teammate did he beat to score his 50th goal?

21) Only two players have ever scored their 500th career goal as a member of the New York Rangers. Both did it in the 1990s. Name both players, and the goalies they beat for their milestone goals.

22) Four individuals who were acquired in trades or signed as free agents by the Rangers recorded their 1,000th career point while playing on Broadway. Can you name all four of them?

23) Drafted 85th overall by New York in 1990, this defenceman led the Rangers in points during the 1993–94 season when he had 89 (12G, 77A). Who was this high-scoring rearguard?
Hint: He has won Stanley Cups with New York (1994) and Dallas (1999).

24) This defenceman holds the Rangers' team record for most assists in one season with 80 helpers during the 1991–92 season. But it was

as a Boston Bruin that he recorded his 1,000th career point during the 2005–06 season. Name him.
Hint: He is the only Ranger to be awarded the Conn Smythe Trophy as the best player in the playoffs.

25) He first joined the Rangers during the 2003–04 season after a trade with Washington and recorded 29 points in 31 games to finish the year. In 2005–06 he set team records for most points in one season (123) and most goals in one season (54). Who is he?

26) This rookie netminder won 30 games for the Rangers in 2005–06, breaking the mark held by legendary goaltenders Johnny Bower and "Sugar" Jim Henry (both of whom won 29 games in their first year). Who is he?

27) This Ranger defenceman was tied (with Ottawa's Wade Redden) for the NHL lead in plus/minus during the 2005–06 season when

Ranger forward Andy Hebenton (#12) tries to score on Boston goaltender Eddie Johnston.

he was a plus-35. Who is he?
Hint: He was signed as a free agent by the Rangers in 2005 after starting his career with the Pittsburgh Penguins.

28) This winger scored his 600th career goal on November 19, 2006, when the Rangers beat Tampa Bay 4–1 at Madison Square Garden. He scored the milestone goal against Lightning netminder Johan Holmqvist. Who is he?

TRADES

1) Even though he was the Rangers' goalie during their Stanley Cup–winning season of 1927–28, Lorne Chabot was dealt to Toronto after he suffered an eye injury in the '28 playoffs. Which goaltender did the Rangers receive in return when the deal was completed on October 18, 1928?

2) On April 16, 1928, the Rangers sent Alex Gray to the Maple Leafs in return for a left winger who would play the rest of his career in New York. He was on the Rangers' Stanley Cup–winning team of 1933 and he led the team in goals scored in 1936–37 (his last full NHL season), when he had 22. Name him.

3) This Toledo, Ohio–born right winger was acquired in a cash deal between the Rangers and Springfield of the Can-Am league on January 1, 1931. He would play on one Stanley Cup team with New York and he recorded 30 or more points for seven straight seasons. He was eventually traded to Detroit along with Eddie Bush in 1940. Who was he?
Hint: He led the Rangers in goals scored three times and finished with 281 goals.

Defenceman Harry Howell (#3) played in 1,160 games with New York — a Ranger club record.

4) This Hall of Fame defenceman was acquired by the Rangers on January 15, 1936, in a deal with the Chicago Blackhawks. New York sent Earl Seibert to Chicago to complete the deal, and the rearguard they acquired helped them to a Stanley Cup in 1940. He twice scored five goals for the Rangers in one season and he had double-digit point totals for his final five years in New York. He retired from the NHL after the 1941–42 season. Who was he?
Hint: He was the Rangers' captain from 1937–38 to 1941–42.

5) The Rangers were very excited when they completed a deal with Providence of the American Hockey League on December 9, 1948, that saw them land a six-foot, one-inch defenceman with lots of promise. He played six seasons in New York but he was not a favourite of the Rangers' crowd at Madison Square Garden. He was dealt to Chicago for

A native of Detroit, Michigan, John Vanbiesbrouck was selected 72nd overall by New York in the 1981 Entry Draft.

defenceman Bill Gadsby in 1954. Who was he? *Hint: He would go on to play for Boston and Toronto and be named to the Hall of Fame.*

6) A July 20, 1953, deal saw the Rangers acquire this netminder from Cleveland of the American Hockey League in exchange for Emile Francis, Neil Strain and cash. He won 29 games for the Rangers in 1953–54 but only played in seven games for the Rangers over the next two years before he finally found a home — and fame — as a Toronto Maple Leaf. Who was he?

7) On July 20, 1954, the Rangers acquired this small right winger (five foot eight, 147 pounds)

for cash from the Maple Leafs. He would lead the New York club in goals scored with 29 in 1954–55 and followed that up with a pair of 18-goal seasons afterwards. His last NHL season was in 1958–59, when he played with Chicago. Who was he?

8) Acquired in a deal for Wally Hergesheimer on June 19, 1956, this centre would have his best NHL season as a Ranger during the 1958–59 season, when he scored 21 goals and totalled 63 points in 70 games. He would be named captain of the Rangers and would also coach them in the early 1960s. Can you name him?

9) When the Rangers acquired winger Dick Duff from the Maple Leafs in February of 1964, they thought he would find his scoring touch once again. But Duff never liked it on Broadway (only seven goals in 43 games played as a Ranger) and on December 22, 1964, he was dealt again — this time to the Montreal Canadiens. Who did the Rangers get back in return?

10) May 18, 1965, saw the Rangers acquire a netminder from Providence of the American Hockey League. To make the deal happen, New York sent four players (Jim Mikol, Marcel Paille, Aldo Guidolin and Sandy McGregor) to the AHL squad. It was a high price to pay, but the Rangers received a future Hall of Famer in return. Who was he?

11) Even though he had scored only two goals (in 49 games played) as a member of the Rangers, this centre who had been picked up from the Montreal Canadiens looked like he still had a future in the Big Apple. However, he was dealt

away on November 29, 1967, to the St. Louis Blues in exchange for veteran forward Ron Stewart. Who did New York send to St. Louis? *Hint: This player became the first star player for the expansion Blues.*

12) June 12, 1968, saw the Rangers re-acquire a left winger who had begun his career with New York in 1959–60. After playing in Montreal (where he won two Stanley Cups) and Minnesota, the Rangers gave up three players (Wayne Hillman, Dan Seguin and Joey Johnston) to get him back. It was a good deal for New York, since he retuned to score 33 goals in 1969–70 and 36 goals in 1970–71. He was dealt to Vancouver in November of 1971. Who was he?

13) The Rangers selected this centre 21st overall in the 1964 Amateur Draft, but he would only play in 31 games (with a goal and two assists) for New York before he was traded along with Sheldon Kannegiesser to the Pittsburgh Penguins on January 26, 1971. Who did the Rangers receive in return?

14) On October 31, 1971, the Rangers sent defenceman Larry Brown to the Detroit Red Wings in exchange for a big (six-foot-one, 196-pound) centre who would play seven seasons in New York, scoring 20 or more goals on three occasions. His final year in New York was 1976–77, and he signed as a free agent with

Los Angeles for his last NHL season in 1977–78. Who was he?

15) He was the captain of the team and had 262 goals in his career as a Ranger, but Vic Hadfield was traded to the Pittsburgh Penguins on May 27, 1974. In return, the Rangers received a defenceman who would play just over two seasons in New York. Who was he?

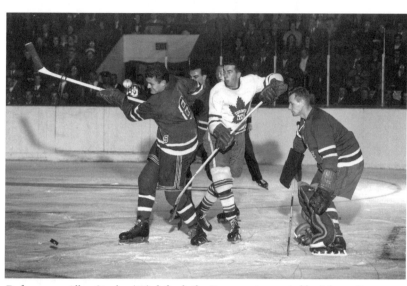

Defenceman Allan Stanley (#8) defends the Ranger net occupied by Johnny Bower.

16) This netminder from Trois-Rivières, Quebec, joined the Rangers for five games during the 1963–64 season and would go on to record 98 career wins for New York. He won 20 or more games four times as a Ranger and shared a Vezina Trophy win with Ed Giacomin in 1971. He was traded to Chicago for Doug Jarrett on October 28, 1975. Who was he?

17) A trade between the Rangers and Bruins on November 7, 1975, shocked the hockey world. No fewer than four star players were involved

in the deal. The Rangers sent Brad Park and Jean Ratelle to Boston in exchange for three players. Name all three players who came to New York in this blockbuster.

18) The Rangers made a major move by sending five players (Pat Hickey, Dean Turner, Lucien DeBlois, Mike McEwen and Bobby Crawford) to the Colorado Rockies on November 2, 1979, to acquire a defenceman who had been drafted second overall in 1977. The big rearguard (six foot three, 216 pounds) had 59 points in his first 61 games as a Ranger, but was never as good again — his next-highest total in New York was only 38. Who was he?

19) Although this NHL superstar was acquired late in his career in a deal with Los Angeles completed March 10, 1987 (Bob Carpenter and Tom Laidlaw went to the Kings), this player scored 31 times and totalled 65 points in 66 games during the 1987–88 season. He then played one more NHL season before retiring. Can you name him?

20) When the Los Angeles Kings decided to move centre Bernie Nicholls (a player who recorded 150 points in 1988–89), they made a deal with the Rangers on January 20, 1990, for a couple of players they hoped would balance their lineup. Which two players did the Rangers give to the Kings?

21) One of the very best trades in Ranger history was

made on October 4, 1991, when the New York club acquired Mark Messier from the Edmonton Oilers. Who did the Rangers send to Edmonton to complete the deal?

22) The Rangers made an important deal when they acquired defenceman Kevin Lowe from the Edmonton Oilers on December 11, 1992. Lowe had won five Stanley Cups with the Oilers and was a vital player when the Rangers won the championship in 1994. Who did the Rangers send to Edmonton to complete a rather one-sided swap?

23) One of the most talented players ever selected by the New York Rangers (15th overall in 1991), Alexei Kovalev was with New York when they won the Stanley Cup in 1994 (recording 21 points in 23 playoff games). The consistent 20-goal scorer was dealt to Pittsburgh on November 25, 1998, along with Harry York, in exchange for three players. Who did the Rangers get back in return?

Goaltender Johnny Bower was a rookie with the New York Rangers in 1953–54.

Defenceman Barry Beck (#3) was New York's captain in 1980–81.

24) Jaromir Jagr was not working out as planned with the Washington Capitals, so they looked for a way to move his big contract. The Rangers proved to be willing partners in a trade. Who did New York send to Washington on January 23, 2004, to complete the transaction?

25) After a long and illustrious career as a Ranger, defenceman Brian Leetch (New York's all-time assist leader with 741) was dealt to the Maple Leafs on March 3, 2004. Who did the Rangers receive in return from Toronto?

26) Signed as a free agent from the Stanley Cup champion Carolina Hurricanes in the summer of 2006, defenceman Aaron Ward did not even last one season with the Rangers before he was dealt to Boston at the trade deadline in 2007. Who did New York get in return?

27) The Rangers drafted Garth Murray 79th overall in 2001, and the tough centre played in just 20 games for New York before he was sent to the Montreal Canadiens in a one-for-one trade. Who did the Rangers get back in return? *Hint: The player the Rangers obtained was selected 16th overall by the Habs in 2000.*

28) Once a high draft choice of the Montreal Canadiens (11th overall in 1997), Jason Ward joined the Rangers for the 2005–06 season as a free agent. He scored 10 goals and had 28 points in 81 games but was traded in the 2006–07 season to the Los Angeles Kings. Which player did the Rangers get back in exchange?

REMEMBER HIM?

1) This Hall of Fame defenceman began his NHL career with the Rangers in 1926–27, scoring three goals and adding two assists in 27 games. In 1927–28, his first full season, he scored 10 times. He was with New York when they won the Stanley Cup in 1928 and 1933 and played in 405 games as a Ranger. He was signed as a free agent by the New York Americans for his final NHL season in 1937–38. Who was he?

2) This defenceman joined the Rangers for the 1931–32 season and was on two (1933 and 1940) Stanley Cup–winning teams before his 647-game career (all played with the Rangers) was over. He never scored more than six goals in one season, but he had double-digit assist totals 12 times (with a career-best 27

helpers in 1943–44). He earned a berth on the NHL's second All-Star team in 1941. Can you name him?

3) These two brothers, born two years apart in Edmonton, Alberta, joined the Rangers for the 1935–36 season. Both played their entire careers in New York and they were teammates on the Rangers' Stanley Cup team of 1940. One brother was elected to the Hall of Fame and had five seasons where he scored in double digits (19 was his highest total). The other brother scored in double digits three times, with 14 being his highest total — a figure he hit on two occasions. Can you name this brother act?

Jaromir Jagr was acquired by the Rangers in a deal with Washington.

4) The Rangers signed this centre/right wing as a free agent for just $4,500 on October 27, 1935, and he would play almost his entire career with New York. He was never a high goal scorer with the Rangers (18 was his highest total, in his final year), but he did lead the NHL in assists in 1941–42, with 37. He was with the Rangers when they won the Stanley Cup in 1940 and joined the Montreal Canadiens for another championship in 1944. After his playing days were over he tried coaching, and was behind the Ranger bench between 1955 and November of 1959. Who was he?

5) This centre joined the Rangers for the 1945–46 season and scored 15 goals, adding 19 assists, good enough to earn him the Calder Trophy as the NHL's top rookie. He had his best year in 1949–50, when he scored 22 goals and had 44 points in 60 games — a performance that gained him the Lady Byng Trophy. He played in exactly 500 games as a Ranger, scoring 108 times and totalling 208 points with only 42 career penalty minutes. Can you name him?

6) This native of Finland (who played his junior hockey in Port Arthur, Ontario) joined the Rangers for the 1948–49 season, and his only real claim to fame was winning the Calder Trophy as the NHL's best rookie after scoring 14 goals and totalling 30 points in 59 games played. He scored 18 times in his second season, but only four in 1950–51. He then played two seasons for the Bruins before leaving the NHL. Who was he?
Hint: He led all playoff scorers in the 1950 post-season with 11 points in 12 games.

7) This centre from Lethbridge, Alberta, started his career with the Rangers in 1958–59 but did

not have his best year until 1961–62, when he scored a career-best 26 goals and 57 points in 70 games played. He became a Pittsburgh Penguin in the expansion season of 1967–68, when he scored 15 times, and he went on to score 21 for the Oakland Seals in 1969–70. He was the coach of the New York Islanders for 30 games in their debut season of 1972–73. Who was he?

New York until the end of the 1973–74 season. His best year in New York came in 1968–69, when he scored 10 goals and totalled 44 points (both career highs). His good play gained him a spot on the NHL's second All-Star team in 1968, and he played in a total 810 games as a Ranger. He ended his career with California and Cleveland. Can you name him?

8) This left winger from Schumacher, Ontario, began his career with the Rangers in 1952–53, when he scored six goals in 55 games played. In 1955–56 he scored 24 goals for New York, a total he topped in 1959–60 with a career-high 32. This consistent performer recorded 422 points as Ranger, including 186 goals. He also played for Boston, Detroit, Pittsburgh and Minnesota. Who was he?

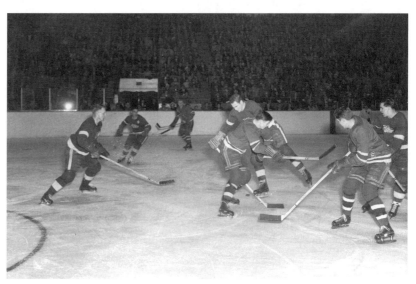

Ranger forward Pentti Lund throws a bodycheck on Detroit's Red Kelly during the 1950 Stanley Cup finals.

9) Born in West Germany on September 29, 1947, this six-foot, 185-pound centre first joined the Rangers for two games in the 1967–68 season. He was a regular the following year and recorded 36 points in 71 games played. He then scored 20 or more goals in five consecutive seasons and recorded 63 or more points over that same time. He finished with 678 points (227G, 451A) in 945 career games, all played as a Ranger. Who was he?

10) This native of Big River, Saskatchewan, became a Ranger in 1962–63, and the large blueliner (six feet, two inches, 205 pounds) stayed in

11) This right winger scored 23 times in 76 games as a rookie with the 1969–70 Rangers, and he followed that up with seasons of 22, 30, 18, 24 and 13 before his career in New York was over. The native of Brandon, Manitoba, was dealt to Minnesota along with Nick Beverley in exchange for Bill Goldsworthy on November 11, 1976. He also played for St. Louis before he retired. Who was he?

12) Drafted 10th overall by the Rangers in 1971, this native of Toronto took the NHL by storm in 1972–73, scoring 30 goals in 61 games and taking away the Calder Trophy as the best

rookie. He had six seasons of 20 or more goals, his highest total being 41 in 1974–75. He scored 246 goals and totalled 586 points in 698 career games — all played as a Ranger. Who was he?

13) On June 18, 1975, the Rangers traded Jerry Butler, Ted Irvine and Bert Wilson to the St. Louis Blues for Bill Collins and this goaltender who had been drafted 5th overall by the Blues in 1973. The big netminder (six foot three, 205 pounds) took the Rangers to the Stanley Cup finals in 1979 and posted 83 victories in a New York uniform, but knee injuries forced him to retire early. Name him.

Defenceman Kevin Lowe (#4) joined the Rangers after a trade with the Edmonton Oilers.

14) This native of Staten Island, New York, did not get his first pair of skates until he was 14 years old. After parts of two seasons in the WHA, he was signed by the Rangers as a free agent on July 23, 1976. He played three seasons in New York, scoring a grand total of nine goals (but recording more than 100 penalty minutes each season). His rights were claimed by the Hartford Whalers in the 1979 Expansion Draft, but the Rangers re-acquired the popular tough guy in 1980–81. He played another four years in New York and twice scored eight goals in a season. He finished with 970 penalty minutes as a Ranger and he had stints with Calgary, Philadelphia and Edmonton before he retired. Who was he?

15) Selected 32nd overall by the Rangers in 1974, this defenceman played his entire 982-game career with New York. He scored 20 or more goals four times and had 40 or more points 10 times. His best year came in 1977–78, when he had 72 points (24 goals, 48 assists) and he had a career-high 27 goals in 1980–81. He finished with 610 points, including 431 assists. Who was he?

16) These two brothers (one a defenceman, the other a left winger) both played for the Rangers in the 1970s and '80s. The left winger was a good goal scorer, potting 20 or more goals five times, while the defenceman was a good set-up man, recording 30 or more points in five consecutive years and usually logging well over 100 minutes in penalties. Both were with the Rangers when they made the Stanley Cup finals in 1979. The winger finished his career with a season in Buffalo, while the defenceman played for Hartford and the New York Islanders before he retired. Can you name them?

17) Drafted 13th overall by New York in 1977, this flamboyant centre/right wing from Sudbury, Ontario, scored 20 goals in 71 games as a rookie in 1977–78. He scored 27, 28 and 17 goals over the next three seasons, before having his best year ever when he found the net 40 times in 1981–82. His output dropped to 19 goals the next year, and he was then traded to Detroit, along with Eddie Mio and Eddie Johnstone, for Mark Osborne, Mike Blaisdell and Willie Huber on June 13, 1983. Name him.

New York goaltender Jacques Plante has defenceman Jim Neilson (#15) and forward Earl Ingarfield (#10) to help him defend against Chicago's Johnny McKenzie.

18) Signed as a free agent after a spectacular career with Winnipeg of the World Hockey Association, this swift right winger scored 33 goals for the Rangers in 1978–79 and totalled 78 points in 80 games played. He never scored fewer than 20 goals in a full season, and he finished with 397 points in 465 NHL games — all played for New York. Who was he?

19) Signed as a free agent by the Rangers on June 5, 1978, this Swedish-born centre scored 27 times in 1978–79 and totalled 66 points in just 59 games played. However, he only got into two playoff games during New York's run to the Stanley Cup finals. He scored 14 goals in each of the next two years, but injuries cut his Ranger career to 170 games in which he recorded 169 points. Who was he?

20) The Rangers sent three players to the Hartford Whalers on October 2, 1981, for this small but slick centre who had recorded 105 points in each of his previous two seasons. In his first season with New York he recorded 103 points (38 goals, 65 assists), and although his production dipped considerably over the next three years (76, 61 and 64 respectively), he remained a valuable player for the New York club. He was dealt to Edmonton in December 1985. Name him.

21) Selected ninth overall by the Rangers in 1981, this defenceman from Winnipeg, Manitoba, began his career in New York during the 1983–84 season. He scored 10 or more goals in seven straight years and had seven consecutive seasons of 40 or more points as a Ranger. His best year in New York saw him record 71 points (14G, 57A) in 80 games. He was traded to the Hartford Whalers in 1993, but not before he had played in 671 games as a Ranger. Who is he?

22) This centre was acquired in a deal with the Detroit Red Wings when the Rangers sent goalie Glen Hanlon to the Motor City. He

scored 24 times in his first year as a Ranger in 1986–87 and followed up with seasons of 23, 26, 22 and 15 before he left New York. San Jose and Calgary were other stops for this player, who recorded 658 points in 761 career games in the NHL. He was also the Rangers' captain prior to Mark Messier. Who was he?

23) Selected 28th overall by the Rangers in 1985, this goaltender from Abington, Pennsylvania, first joined New York for the 1989 playoffs. He won 20 or more games in 10 seasons, and holds the Ranger team record with 301 victories. He backstopped New York to the Stanley Cup in 1994 and spent his entire career as a Ranger. Who was he?

24) This big defenceman (six foot five, 230 pounds) was acquired by the Rangers when they sent David Shaw to Edmonton on November 12, 1991. His experience as a three-time Stanley Cup winner with the Oilers was highly valued by the New York club, and he helped the Rangers win the championship in 1994 (chipping in six assists in 22 post-season games). He recorded over 100 penalty minutes five times as a Ranger, and his highest point total in New York was 19 in 1992–93. A head injury ended his career in 1999. Can you name him?

25) Picking up this pesky left winger from Finland cost the Rangers the services of Doug Weight in a trade with Edmonton on March 17, 1993. His first full season in New York, 1993–94, saw him score 22 goals and total 54 points in 83 games, and he added eight points (4G, 4A) in 23 playoff games as the Rangers took the Stanley Cup. He was gone to St. Louis the following year. Who was he?

26) This former Ranger coach, who guided the team to a record of 131–113–41 between 1981 and 1985, was named to the Hockey Hall of Fame in 2006. Who was he?
Hint: He was named to the United States Hockey Hall of Fame in 1990.

27) Drafted 20th overall by Edmonton in 1991, this well-travelled left winger made three stops with the Rangers — the first coming in 2001–02, when he had 13 points in 15 games, the second in 2003–04, when he counted 42 points in 69 games, and finally in 2005–06, when he had 55 points (16 goals, 39 assists) in just 52 games played. He has also played for Colorado, Montreal, Dallas, St. Louis and Vancouver. Who is he?

Mike Rogers had 308 points in 316 games as a New York Ranger between 1981 and 1986.

28) Pittsburgh drafted this Czech-born centre 19th overall in 1992. In August of 2005 he signed as a free agent with New York and went on to score 22 goals and record 76 points in 2005–06. In addition to the Penguins, he has also played for the Senators, Islanders, Panthers and Kings. Who is he?

New York's Kelly Kisio (#11) tries to establish a position in front of the Toronto net. Kisio was captain of the Rangers between 1988 and 1991.

DID YOU KNOW?

1) The Rangers' original owner was a legendary boxing promoter from Texas named George "Tex" Rickard, and it was he who decided on the nickname for his new NHL team, which began play in 1926–27. Why did he choose "Rangers"?

2) Between 1920 and 1971, the Rangers played a game on Christmas Day 38 times. In fact, a New York game on December 25 became something of a tradition until the practice was stopped entirely by the NHL. Of those 38 games, how many did the Rangers win?
   a) 15 b) 20 c) 25

3) He was the first player in NHL history to record 250 career assists when the Rangers defeated the New York Americans 7–5 on March 9, 1937. Which player established the mark?
   Hint: He is an Honoured Member of the Hall of Fame.

4) Only two New York Ranger goaltenders have ever recorded 10 or more shutouts in one season. They both played for the team early in its history. Who were they?

5) On January 16, 1936, the Rangers defeated the Maple Leafs 1–0. The only goal came on a penalty shot — the first-ever successful attempt in team history. The player who scored the goal missed on two previous attempts but finally scored on George Hainsworth. Who was he?
   Hint: This player would play only 72 games as a Ranger (scoring a total of 12 goals) but would go on to play on Chicago's Stanley Cup–winning team of 1938.

6) While a member of the Detroit Red Wings, this goalie was loaned to the Rangers for one period of play on December 23, 1943, when regular Ranger netminder Ken McAuley was injured. The Red Wings won the game 5–3, but the replacement goalkeeper did not give up a goal. By appearing in this game for the Rangers, the goalie in question played for five of the six "Original Six" teams. Who was he?
   Hint: The only team he did not play for was Montreal.

7) A January 20, 1954, contest between the Rangers and the Bruins was unusual for New York coach Muzz Patrick, because when he looked at the Boston bench he saw a very familiar face. Who was the Bruins' coach that night?

8) On January 27, 1955, Gordie Howe took 19 shots on net during one game against the New York Rangers. Even though he outshot the entire Ranger team (who mustered only 18 shots on the Detroit net), he did not record a goal or an assist. The game ended in a 3–3 tie, and one of the New York goals came from the stick of a player who scored only three times his entire NHL career. His identity becomes even more ironic considering Howe's futility on this night. Who was the Ranger forward in question?

Goaltender Mike Richter (#35) holds the team record for most career wins with 301.

9) The Rangers were not a very good team for most of the decade of the 1950s, missing the playoffs on numerous occasions. Lorne "Gump" Worsley suffered the most as the Rangers' netminder for many of those years. On one occasion he was asked which team gave him the most trouble. What was his surprising response?

10) This goaltender played two periods of a game for the Rangers at Maple Leaf Gardens on February 3, 1962, replacing Gump Worsley, who was injured during the contest. The substitute goalie allowed three goals and the Leafs beat the Rangers 4–1. He went on to play for Chicago, Buffalo and Edmonton, winning a total of 66 NHL games. Who was he?
Hint: He had a famous brother who was also a netminder.

11) On December 15, 1962, this Ranger scored a goal in a 4–2 victory over Montreal, and he also scored at least once in each of the next nine games (notching a total of 11 goals) before the Canadiens snapped his streak by holding him scoreless in a game on January 6, 1963. Who holds this Ranger club record?

12) Looking for any possible way to improve their team, the Rangers signed this Swedish forward as a free-agent in October 1964. The one-time member of the Swedish national team played in just four games for the Rangers in 1964–65, without registering a point. He then decided to go back home. Can you name him?

13) This former Montreal Canadien great was dissatisfied with retirement. The Rangers claimed him on waivers on June 9, 1966, and

Muzz Patrick was coach of the Rangers in 1953–54 and 1954–55 and again in 1962–63.

'76." The Rangers hosted one of the games at Madison Square Garden on December 28, 1975, against the Soviet Red Army team. What was the result of this international exhibition game?

16) Known as the GAG Line, this trio set a team record by scoring a combined 133 goals and recording a total of 302 points during the 1971–72 season. Who were the members of this high-scoring line, and what did "GAG" stand for?

17) Signed as a free agent by the Rangers on September 12, 1983, this talented but free-spirited centre had played for Pittsburgh, Montreal and Hartford before he took his act to Broadway. He set a Ranger team record for most goals in a season by a centre with 48 in 1983–84, and he would score 24, 20 and 28 goals in the following three seasons. He had 12 points in 10 games to finish his career in 1987–88. Who was he?

the former 50-goal scorer played the 1966–67 season with them, scoring 17 goals and 25 assists and helping them make the playoffs. He scored five goals in 59 games the next year before retiring for good. Who was he?

14) This Ranger right winger had the honour of being the first player in team history to have his sweater number retired on March 9, 1977, prior to a 6–4 win by New York over the Minnesota North Stars. Which player was honoured that night?

15) During the Christmas holiday period in 1975, two Soviet club teams embarked on a tour of NHL cities in what was called "Super Series

18) When this former Montreal Canadien superstar asked Ranger general manager Phil Esposito for a tryout, Espo felt he could not turn down the retired Hab. The right winger made the team and recorded 18 goals and 27 assists in 1988–89. He then signed with the Quebec Nordiques for the following season. Can you name him?

19) Drafted 68th overall by the Rangers in 1988, Tony Amonte was a speedy right winger who scored 35 goals in 1991–92, his first full season in New York. He had 33 a year later, but after scoring 16 times in 72 games during the 1993–94 campaign, he was dealt to Chicago for two players. Who were they?

20) On March 21, 1994, the Rangers sent Todd Marchant to Edmonton in return for this centre, who helped them win the Stanley Cup. He would only play 12 regular-season games (recording six points) for the Rangers and 23 in the '94 playoffs (five points) before moving on to the Philadelphia Flyers. In 2006 he coached the Oilers to the Stanley Cup finals. Who is he?

Hint: He took the final face-off in the Ranger zone to close out the seventh game of the 1994 Stanley Cup finals against Vancouver.

Ranger netminder Gump Worsley makes a save against the Maple Leafs. Worsley won 20 or more games seven times as a Ranger.

21) Only three men have ever coached the Rangers to a Stanley Cup title. The great Lester Patrick did it twice, in 1928 and 1933. Can you name the other two championship mentors?

22) Signed as a free agent in 1996, The Great One, Wayne Gretzky, recorded 97 points (including a league-leading 72 assists) his first year in New York. He led the NHL in assists once again in 1997–98, with 67, but he decided to retire at the conclusion of the 1998–99 season. His final game was played at Madison Square Garden on April 18, 1999, in a 2–1 loss to the Pittsburgh Penguins. How did Gretzky do in his last NHL contest?

23) After much deliberation, the Rangers finally decided to take a risk and send a package of players to Philadelphia to acquire Eric Lindros. The large centre would score 37 goals in his first season in New York, but only 19 the following year and then 10 in 39 games during 2003–04. He signed with Toronto as a free agent in 2005. Who did the Rangers send to the Flyers to complete the deal on August 20, 2001?

24) A March 18, 2002, deal saw the Rangers send a package of players and draft choices to the Florida Panthers in exchange for an exciting right winger who had scored 50 goals five times in his career to that point. He notched 12 goals in his first 12 games as a Ranger to close the 2001–02 season. The flashy winger scored 19 times in 39 games the following year, but a previous knee injury returned to end his career at that point. Who was he?

25) Drafted 204th overall by the Rangers in 2002, this right winger had one of the best rookie seasons in team history when he scored 30 goals in 2005–06. Who is he?

26) The Rangers had a very good year in 2005–06, when they won 44 games and recorded a total of 100 points. The team won 25 games at home and came up with a unique way of thanking the fans after each of these home-ice victories. What did the Rangers do to acknowledge the New York fans?

27) This native of Minnesota was never a big goal scorer until the 2005–06 season, when he scored 25 for the Stanley Cup champion Carolina Hurricanes. The Rangers then signed the centre as a free agent, but he was not as productive in 2006–07. He also played for the Mighty Ducks of Anaheim. Who is he?

28) Signed as a free agent by the Rangers in 2004, this Swedish-born centre scored 23 goals and added 56 assists for 79 points (the second-best mark on the team next to Jaromir Jagr) in 2005–06. In 2006–07 he had 83 points (26 goals and 57 assists) in 79 games. He has also played for Hartford, Calgary, Tampa Bay, Chicago, Washington and Boston during his NHL career. Who is he?

Andy Bathgate (#9) poses with Larry Popein and Dean Prentice (#17).

TORONTO MAPLE LEAFS

A common sight in the 1960s: Maple Leaf captain George Armstrong holding the Stanley Cup.

MEMORABLE GAMES

1) The first game ever played at Maple Leaf Gardens took place on November 12, 1931, when the Maple Leafs played the Chicago Blackhawks. The final game played in the same building took place on February 13, 1999, also against Chicago. What was the result of each game, and which Blackhawk players scored the first- and last-ever goals at the Gardens?

2) The Maple Leafs won their first Stanley Cup (in their first season in Maple Leaf Gardens) on home ice on the night of April 9, 1932. Which three teams did the Leafs beat to win the Cup, and which player scored the winning goal in the final contest?

3) April 3, 1933, was a long night at the Gardens as the Maple Leafs played the longest game in team history. It was the deciding game of a semi-final playoff series against Boston, and it took 104:26 of extra play to decide the issue. The Leafs got a goal from an unexpected source to win the game and take the best-of-five series three games to two. Who scored the winner?

4) During the 1942 Stanley Cup finals, the Maple Leafs staged the most dramatic comeback in sports history when they won the last four games of the series after losing the first three. The final

contest was played at the Gardens on April 18. Pete Langelle scored the Cup winner in the 3–1 Leaf victory, but another Leaf got both of the other Toronto goals. Who was he?

5) In 1945, the Maple Leafs took the first three games of the Stanley Cup finals against Detroit, only to lose the games four through six. It looked as if the comeback scenario of 1942 might repeat itself, but in reverse. The seventh and deciding game was played at the Detroit Olympia on April 22. It was a tight game and the Leafs took advantage of a power-play opportunity to score the winner. Who got this important marker?

6) On April 19, 1947, the Maple Leafs won the Stanley Cup on home ice by beating the Canadiens 2–1 in the sixth game of the series. The player who scored the winning goal scored three times in the finals, helping a very young Toronto team win the championship. Who was he?

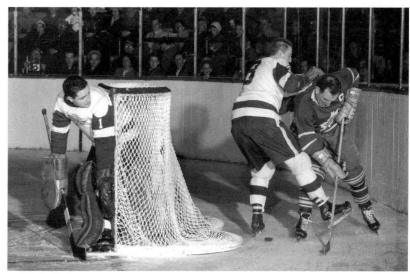

Captain Ted Kennedy battles Marcel Pronovost behind the Detroit net. Kennedy was named captain of the Leafs when Syl Apps retired.

7) The fourth game of the 1948 Stanley Cup finals, played at Detroit's Olympia on April 14, 1948, saw this great Leaf player score the final goal of his outstanding career. The Leafs whipped the Red Wings 7–2 that night to sweep the series in four straight games. Which Leaf scored his final NHL tally in this contest?

Dick Duff (middle of photo) looks up to find the puck against the Detroit Red Wings. Duff scored many important goals against Detroit during his career as a Leaf.

8) The Maple Leafs finished in fourth place during the regular season in 1948–49, but they came on strong in the playoffs to beat Boston (in five games) and Detroit (in four) to become the first team in NHL history to win the Stanley Cup in three consecutive seasons. The final game of the final series was played on April 16 at the Gardens, and Toronto beat the Red Wings 3–1. Who scored the Cup-clinching goal?

9) The Maple Leafs and Canadiens staged one of the most memorable Stanley Cup finals in 1951, when every game of the series went into over-time. The Leafs were up three games to one when they returned home to play the fifth game at the Gardens on April 21. Toronto pulled out a 3–2 overtime win on Bill Barilko's famous goal — sadly, the last of his career. The Habs nearly won the contest, and the Leafs had to pull their goalie in the last minute to try for the tying goal. Who scored this key goal late in the third period?

10) On March 16, 1957, the Leafs set a team record by scoring 14 times during a home game against the New York Rangers. Toronto took the contest 14–1, and two Leafs paced the team by recording hat tricks. Which players had the three-goal games, and which Ranger netminder gave up all the goals?

11) The Maple Leafs trailed the New York Rangers by seven points in the NHL standings with only five games to play late in the 1958–59 season, but they staged a miraculous rally to secure the last playoff spot available on the final night of the season. On March 22, the Leafs were in Detroit in a must-win situation. Though the Wings jumped out to a 2–0 lead, the score was eventually tied at 4–4. This winger scored to put the Leafs ahead 5–4, and they eventually won by a 6–4 count. On the same night, another team helped Toronto's cause by beating the Rangers. Who scored the winning goal for the Leafs, and which team helped them out?

12) The first time a player scored two short-handed goals in one playoff game came on

April 18, 1963, when the Leafs clinched the Stanley Cup on home ice with a 3–1 victory over the Detroit Red Wings. Who scored the two markers while the Leafs were down a man, and what were the added circumstances around the second of the two goals?

13) On April 23, 1964, a crowd of 15,222 fans jammed the Detroit Olympia hoping to see the hometown Red Wings clinch their first Stanley Cup title since 1955. Maple Leaf defenceman Bob Baun broke their hearts by scoring a game-winning goal at 1:43 of extra time — while skating with a broken bone in his leg — to give the Leafs a 4–3 win. The Leafs battled back all game long and made it 3–3 late in the second period on a goal by a player who was not normally getting a lot of ice time under coach Punch Imlach. Who scored this important goal at 17:48 of the second?

14) The night of April 25, 1964, saw the Maple Leafs win their third straight Stanley Cup with a 4–0 victory over the Red Wings at Maple Leaf Gardens. Andy Bathgate opened the scoring for Toronto early in the first period, and the score remained 1–0 until 4:26 of the third period, when the Leafs broke the tension and added another goal. They pumped in two more in the final stanza to make it a resounding win over Detroit. Which Leafs scored the third-period markers?

15) With the Maple Leafs leading the Montreal Canadiens 2–1 with less than a minute to play on May 2, 1967, coach Punch Imlach sent out a veteran group of players to preserve the victory and give the Leafs their fourth Stanley Cup of the 1960s. Name all the Leafs' players on the ice. Which one took the face-off in the Toronto end, and which one scored the goal?

16) The Maple Leafs had virtually no chance of beating the Boston Bruins when they met in the first round of the playoffs in 1972. Predictably, they were eliminated in five games. The lone Leaf victory came at the

Dave Keon (#14) was the Leafs' most consistent player in the 1967 playoffs, when they beat Chicago and Montreal.

Boston Garden in the second game of the series, played on April 6, on an overtime marker that gave the Leafs a 4–3 win. Which Leaf scored the goal?
Hint: He was a former Bruin who had been acquired by the Leafs for Wayne Carleton.

One of the toughest players to wear a Leaf uniform, Bobby Baun (#21).

they played host to the Philadelphia Flyers, who held a 3–2 lead in games in their quarter-final playoff series. The Flyers had the edge in goal with Bernie Parent, but on this night the Leafs had his number, and their 8–5 triumph forced a seventh game. Which Leaf scored five goals in this game?

17) When Darryl Sittler had his record-setting 10-point night (six goals, four assists) against the Boston Bruins on February 7, 1976, one other Leaf player had a big night as well, with two goals and two assists. Who was he?

18) On Darryl Sittler's recording-breaking night of February 7, 1976, Dave Reece (who never played in the NHL again) was in the Boston net. On the Bruins' bench that night was a future Hall of Fame netminder who had just returned to the team from the World Hockey Association and wanted no part of replacing Reece that magical night. Who was he?
Hint: He was a former Maple Leaf netminder.

19) The night of April 22, 1976, saw the Maple Leafs on the brink of elimination. That night,

20) The Maple Leafs won their first seven-game playoff series since the 1967 finals on the night of April 29, 1978, when Lanny McDonald (playing with a broken nose and an injured wrist) scored at 4:13 of overtime to knock off the New York Islanders 2–1 and clinch a hard-fought quarter-final series. Which Leaf scored the other goal in the contest?

21) May 1, 1993, is a night few Maple Leaf fans will ever forget, as the team rallied to tie the seventh game of the Norris Division semi-final, 3–3, late in regulation time. The Leafs then scored at 2:35 of the extra session on a point shot that was redirected into the Detroit net for the winner. Who scored to tie the game, and which Leaf won it in overtime?

22) The Maple Leafs played in Los Angeles on the night of May 27, 1993, with a chance to advance to the Stanley Cup finals for the first time since 1967. They tied the game 4–4 with a late goal (the player's third of the night), but lost in overtime when the Kings scored a power-play goal. Who had the hat trick for the Leafs, and which Leaf player took a penalty to give Los Angeles the extra man?

23) The Maple Leafs were hopeful of making the Stanley Cup finals in 1994 when they met the Vancouver Canucks in the Western Conference finals, but they lost the series in

five games. The lone Leaf victory came on home ice during the first game of the series, played on May 16. Peter Zezel scored in overtime to give the Leafs a 3–2 victory. Which Vancouver netminder did he beat for his winning tally?

24) The Maple Leafs have not had much success against the Philadelphia Flyers in the playoffs, but they finally won a series against Philadelphia — in six games — in 1999. The final contest was played in Philadelphia on May 2, and the Leafs got a goal very late in regulation time to win 1–0. Who scored the goal?

25) Mats Sundin has had many great nights as a Maple Leaf, but none has been more

Defenceman Pavel Kubina scored seven goals for the Leafs in 2006–07.

memorable than the game played on October 14, 2006, at the Air Canada Centre, in which Sundin scored three times to give Toronto a 5–4 overtime victory. Which goalie allowed all three goals, and what was significant about the final tally?

26) The Maple Leafs couldn't seem to get the hang of the shootout during the 2005–06 season, winning only three of the 10 they took part in. But on October 24, 2005, at the Air Canada Centre, they won their first shootout by beating Boston 5–4. Who scored the winner for the Leafs, and which Bruin goalie did he beat?

27) Alex Steen had a very good rookie season with the Maple Leafs in 2005–06, when he scored 18 goals and totalled 45 points. On October 8, 2005, the native of Winnipeg, Manitoba, got off to a good start when he scored his first NHL goal in a 5–4 loss to Montreal at the Air Canada Centre. Which Canadien goalie did Steen score on?

28) On February 17, 2006, the Maple Leafs celebrated their 80th anniversary and invited a special group of players to help them celebrate the event. Who made up the group, and which team did the Leafs beat 4–3 at the Air Canada Centre that night?

RECORDS AND AWARDS

1) He was the first Maple Leaf to score five goals in a game, when Toronto beat the New York Americans 11–3 at Maple Leaf Gardens on January 19, 1932. Who was he?
Hint: He led the NHL in goals scored a total of five times in the 1930s.

2) This player set a team record by scoring four goals in one period when the Maple Leafs beat the St. Louis Eagles 5–2 on November 20, 1934. He also holds the team record for most nominations to the NHL's first All-Star team (a total of four times). Who was he?

3) Only three players have played on five Maple Leaf Stanley Cup–winning teams. Two of the best known were goalie Turk Broda and centre Ted Kennedy. Who was the third?

4) Only two Leafs have ever won the Hart Trophy as the NHL's most valuable player. Name both of them.

5) This right winger set an NHL record for rookies by scoring five goals in one game when the Maple Leafs whipped the Chicago Blackhawks 10–4 on January 8, 1947, at the Gardens. The record has only been matched once since then. Who scored the five markers for Toronto? *Hint: He also holds the Maple Leafs' team record for the two fastest power-play goals, scored within six seconds of each other in a game against Montreal on February 9, 1952.*

6) He scored just 14 goals as a rookie (to go along with 13 assists) for the Maple Leafs in 1965–66 but was still able to win the Calder Trophy as the best newcomer to the NHL. Who was he?

7) He set an NHL record by scoring two goals for the Maple Leafs after just 1:08 of a playoff game against the Red

Wings in 1963 and also notched the Stanley Cup–winning goal on April 22, 1962, when the Leafs beat Chicago 2–1 to give them their first championship of the 1960s. Who was he?

8) These two Maple Leaf netminders became the first goalies in NHL history to share the Vezina Trophy when they won it in 1965. Who are they?

9) Goaltender Terry Sawchuk was best remembered as a Maple Leaf for his performance in the 1967 playoffs, when Toronto won the Stanley Cup. However, he achieved another milestone with the Leafs on the night of March 4, 1967, when Toronto beat Chicago 3–0. What was significant about that shutout?

10) On January 2, 1971, the Maple Leafs registered their highest shutout score when they won the contest played at the Gardens by a scored of 13–0. That game also saw them score seven

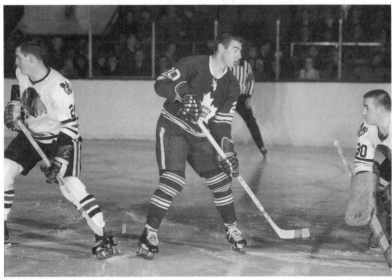

Bob Pulford (#20) was at his best in the playoffs during his career as a Maple Leaf.

times in the second period — also a team record for most goals in one period. Which opponent did the Leafs beat in this game?

11) How many players have played 1,000 games in a Maple Leaf uniform?
a) 3 b) 4 c) 5

12) On February 2, 1977, Detroit goalies Jim Rutherford (two) and Ed Giacomin (three) allowed a record five goals by a Maple Leaf defenceman. The game was played at the Gardens, and Toronto won the contest 9–1. Who was the Leaf blueliner?
Hint: This player also scored four goals in one game as a member of the Los Angeles Kings in 1981.

Borje Salming (#21) was a six-time NHL All-Star with the Maple Leafs.

13) He led the Maple Leafs in penalty minutes six straight seasons between 1974–75 and 1979–80 and would go on to to become the NHL's all-time leader in penalty minutes (4,421 in his career). Who was he?

14) The game the Maple Leafs played on the road on the night of March 18, 1981, was one they would rather forget. Toronto gave up a team-record number of goals in a 14–4 shellacking. Where was the game played?

15) On January 8, 1986, the Maple Leafs were involved in the second-highest-scoring game in team history when they won 11–9 on home ice. Who was the opposition, and which Leaf scored four goals in the game?

16) The night of January 8, 1944, saw Leaf defenceman Walter "Babe" Pratt set a team record with six assists during a 12–3 victory over the Boston Bruins. Which Leaf tied this mark when Toronto beat Minnesota 6–1 on February 13, 1993, at the Gardens?

17) Darryl Sittler holds the Leafs' team record for most points in one game (10) but who holds the next highest mark for a single game?

18) Six Maple Leaf players have recorded exactly six points in one game. Four were centres, one was a right winger and the other a defenceman. Can you name all of them?

19) There have not been many 50-goal seasons in Maple Leafs history; only three different players have reached the plateau, for a total of six times. Name all three players.

The 1966–67 Maple Leafs' two legendary goalies: Terry Sawchuk and Johnny Bower.

20) Only two players have ever recorded 100 or more points in a season for the Maple Leafs. Can you name both, and which was the first to hit the magic mark?

21) Although he did not win the Calder Trophy as the NHL's top rookie in 1985–86, when he had 34 goals, Wendel Clark *was* named rookie of the year by *The Sporting News* (as chosen by the players) and *The Hockey News* (as selected by the fans). Behind which player did Clark finish second in the Calder Trophy voting?

22) Six players have recorded their 1,000th career point while wearing a Maple Leaf uniform. Can you name all of them?
Hint: None of these players began their NHL careers with Toronto.

23) Only one Maple Leaf bench boss has ever won the Jack Adams Award as the NHL's coach of the year, and only one has been named runner-up. Can you name both, and the years involved?

24) Only two coaches in Maple Leafs history have won 300 games with the team. Name both of them.

25) The 2006–07 season saw Mats Sundin rack up at least 20 goals for the 12th time as a Leaf, establishing a new team record. Two other Leafs posted 11 seasons of 20 or more goals. Who were they?

26) Drafted 12th overall by Colorado in 1994, this rugged winger (and sometime defenceman)

was picked up by the Maple Leafs on waivers from Calgary in February of 2001. While he is not a skilled player, he has played the enforcer role very well for Toronto, and in 2006–07 he registered the 1,000th penalty minute of his career. Who is this tough guy?

27) During a pre-game ceremony on October 4, 2006, the Maple Leafs added three more names to their list of players whose numbers are honoured (though not retired). Who were the three players added to a very select group?

28) Even though his performance in 2006–07 was somewhat inconsistent, this Leaf goaltender played in 72 games — the second-highest total in team history (only two games away from Felix Potvin's 74 appearances in 1996–97). He also tied a team record (established by Ed Belfour in 2002–03) by winning 37 games. Can you name this Toronto netminder?

TRADES

1) One of the first major trades made by Conn Smythe came to pass on October 10, 1930, when he sent two players — Art Smith and Eric Pettinger — and $35,000 in cash (a huge amount at the time) to the Ottawa Senators for a colourful defenceman. Who was he?

Toronto defenceman Tim Horton tries to block the path of Detroit's Red Kelly (wearing the "C" on his Red Wing sweater). Rudy Migay is the other Leaf in the photo.

2) The Maple Leafs made a very shrewd move when they sent four players to the New York Americans in 1939 for Dave "Sweeney" Schriner, a gifted goal scorer who would play a big part in helping the Leafs win the Stanley Cup in 1942. Which players did Toronto send to New York to complete the deal?

3) Maple Leaf manager Conn Smythe, who was away at the time on military service, was very upset when he learned that a defenceman had been traded to the Montreal Canadiens on February 28, 1943, for the rights to Ted Kennedy. But it turned out to be one of the best deals Toronto ever made, and Smythe would one day call Kennedy the best Maple Leaf of all time. Who did the Leafs send to Montreal to complete a one-sided deal?

4) The Maple Leafs shocked the hockey world when they sent a total of five players — Gaye Stewart, Bud Poile, Gus Bodnar, Bob Goldham and Ernie Dickens — all of whom had been on

a Stanley Cup winner in Toronto, to Chicago for two players on November 2, 1947. Which two players did the Leafs get in return?

5) The Maple Leafs were looking to add a veteran defenceman to their roster in October of 1958 and sent another veteran blueliner — Jim Morrison (399 games as a Leaf) — to the Boston Bruins to complete a swap. The Leafs put their new acquisition alongside Tim Horton, and Toronto had a steady defence pair that would play together for a decade. Who was he?

6) Toronto general manager and coach Punch Imlach made a small but significant deal with the New York Rangers in November of 1960 when he sent wingers Pat Hannigan and Johnny Wilson to Broadway in exchange for one player. The rambunctious winger the Leafs received in return would play on four Stanley Cup teams in Toronto. Can you name him?

Wendel Clark (#17) scored 260 goals in 608 games as a Maple Leaf.

7) Marc Reaume was a little-known defenceman who had played in 267 games (scoring eight goals and adding 39 assists) for the Maple Leafs between 1954–55 and 1959–60, but he found himself in the middle of perhaps the greatest deal in team history. Reaume was sent to Detroit on February 10, 1960, in exchange for a defenceman the Leafs would convert into a centre. Who did the Leafs get from the Red Wings?

8) The New York Rangers were interested in adding younger players to their team and knew that the Maple Leafs wanted to add some veteran help to try for a third straight Stanley Cup in 1964. Toronto sent Dick Duff, Bob Nevin, Arnie Brown, Rod Seiling and Bill

Collins to the Rangers in exchange for two players on February 22, 1964. Who were they?

9) A May 20, 1965, deal saw fan favourite Billy Harris sent to Detroit along with Andy Bathgate and Gary Jarrett in return for five players. Three of these players would help Toronto win the Stanley Cup in 1967. Can you name all five?
Hint: One player was a defenceman who would go on to be elected to the Hall of Fame.

10) Punch Imlach had told Detroit Red Wing speedster Paul Henderson that he would try to get him in a deal one day, and on March 3, 1968, that prophecy came true. Norm Ullman and journeyman Floyd Smith came with

Henderson to the Maple Leafs in a multi-player deal that shocked everyone in the city of Toronto. Who did the Leafs send to Detroit?

11) Pierre Pilote had been one of the best defencemen in the NHL during the decade of the 1960s (three straight Norris Trophies), but his career was essentially over by 1968. The Leafs foolishly sent a young right winger to Chicago to acquire Pilote, who would only play one season as a Leaf. Who did the Leafs give away to the Blackhawks?
Hint: He had scored the Stanley Cup–winning goal for the Leafs in 1967.

12) A February 1, 1971, deal saw the Leafs send journeyman goalie Bruce Gamble and flashy

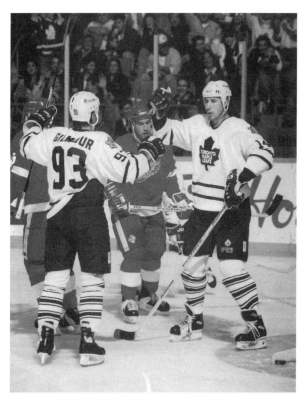

Dave Andreychuk (#14) scored 120 goals in 223 games as a Maple Leaf.

forward Mike Walton, along with a first-round pick (who turned out to be Pierre Plante), to Philadelphia in exchange for a netminder and a second-round draft selection. Who was the goalie the Leafs received in return, and who did they take with the draft choice?

13) In exchange for the rights to one of the greatest players in Maple Leafs history, Toronto received Denis Dupere, Guy Trottier and Jacques Plante via the New York Rangers on March 3, 1970. Who was the Leaf player involved in the transaction?
Hint: He would go on to play for Pittsburgh and Buffalo.

14) When the Bruins were looking for a veteran netminder to help out during the stretch drive and playoffs in 1972–73, the Leafs were able to take advantage by sending goalie Jacques Plante and a third-round pick (Doug Gibson) to Boston in return for a first-round draft choice in 1973 and a player to be named later. Who did the Leafs select with their pick, and who was the player to be named later?

15) When Bernie Parent decided he wanted to return to the NHL after a brief stint in the World Hockey Association, he did not wish to play for Toronto — the team that owned his rights — again. He was accommodated with a trade back to Philadelphia, along with a second-round pick in 1973 (the Flyers took Larry Goodenough), in return for a first-round draft choice in 1973 and a veteran netminder who was named later. Who did the Leafs select, and which goalie eventually ended up in Toronto?

Doug Gilmour was acquired by the Maple Leafs in a trade with the Calgary Flames.

16) The Maple Leafs had high hopes when they selected Don Ashby (1975) and Trevor Johansen (1977) in the first rounds of their respective drafts, but both were sent to the Colorado Rockies on March 13, 1979, for this centre who Toronto hoped would add some scoring to their team. Who was he?

17) A vindictive Punch Imlach (he was feuding with many Toronto players upon his return as Leafs general manager in the summer of 1979) traded Lanny McDonald and defenceman Joel Quenneville to the Colorado Rockies on December 29, 1979, in return for two players who did not last very long as Maple Leafs. Who were they?

18) Dave "Tiger" Williams was one of the toughest and most determined Maple Leafs ever to wear the uniform, but he was still traded, along with checking winger Jerry Butler, to the Vancouver Canucks on February 18, 1980, in return for two players who had been first-round draft choices. Name both players the Leafs received in return.

19) When it was finally completed, a January 20, 1982, deal saw the Leafs get Rich Costello, Ken Strong and Peter Ihnacak (selected by the Leafs with a draft choice) from Philadelphia in exchange for which player?
Hint: The player the Leafs gave up was a future Hall of Famer.

20) Defenceman Al Iafrate had all the necessary physical skills to be a great player, and the Maple Leafs thought so highly of the Michigan native that they selected him fourth overall in 1984. While he showed flashes of greatness (22 goals one year), Iafrate never really lived up to his promise. The Leafs traded him to Washington for two very useful players. Who did the Leafs get back in return?

21) When Cliff Fletcher took over as general manager of the Maple Leafs in 1991, he quickly put his mark on the team by sending Vincent Damphousse, Luke Richardson, Scott Thornton and Peter Ing to the Edmonton Oilers in return for three players. Who did Fletcher get back in return?

22) In a blockbuster deal completed on January 2, 1992, the fortunes of the Maple Leafs changed completely when they acquired Doug Gilmour, Jamie Macoun, Ric Nattress, Rick Wamsley and Kent Manderville from the

Calgary Flames in a deal engineered by Toronto general manager Cliff Fletcher. Who did the Leafs give up?

23) Maple Leaf fans were unanimously shocked when Toronto captain Wendel Clark was dealt to the Quebec Nordiques on June 28, 1994. Defenceman Sylvain Lefebvre and prospect Landon Wilson, along with a first-round pick, also went to Quebec in a deal that changed the Leaf team significantly. Who did the Leafs get in return?

24) When Doug Gilmour decided he did not want to re-sign with the Maple Leafs in 1997, general manager Cliff Fletcher sent him to New Jersey for three players. Can you name all three?

The Maple Leafs made a great deal when they got fan favourite Eddie Shack in a trade with the New York Rangers.

25) Darcy Tucker was picked up in a deal with the Tampa Bay Lightning on February 9, 2000. Name the two players the Leafs sent to the Lightning.

26) Although he played very well in 466 games for the Maple Leafs in the 1990s, defenceman Jamie Macoun was near the end of his playing days when Toronto sent him to Detroit on March 24, 1998. He won the Stanley Cup with the Red Wings in 1998, when he played in 22 post-season games, scoring twice and adding two assists. In return for Macoun, the Leafs received a fourth-round draft choice. Who did the Leafs take with that pick?
Hint: He scored 21 goals for the Leafs in both 2005–06 and 2006–07.

27) Originally drafted by the Washington Capitals (177th overall) in 1990, defenceman Ken Klee was signed by the Maple Leafs as a free agent in September of 2003. He played well for Toronto in the early part of the 2003–04 season and finished with 29 points in 66 regular-season games. In 2005–06 he had 15 points in 56 games before he was dealt to New Jersey for a minor-league winger. Who is he?

28) When the Maple Leafs drafted goaltender Mikael Tellqvist 70th overall in 2000, they thought the goaltender of the future was in the fold. His play in the 2005–06 season (a 10–11–2 record) showed that this was not going to be the case, so he was dealt to Phoenix early in the 2006–07 season. Who did the Leafs get back in return?
Hint: He was drafted by the Vancouver Canucks, but never played for them. He spent at least 100 minutes in the penalty box in each of five seasons with the St. Louis Blues.

REMEMBER HIM?

1) One of the biggest (six feet, 190 pounds) and toughest players of his era, this Toronto defenceman led the NHL in penalty minutes for eight straight seasons between 1932–33 and 1939–40, and he scored a career-high 11 goals in 1933–34. He played in seven Stanley Cup finals with the Maple Leafs, winning the championship in 1932. In all, he played in 490 regular-season games as a Leaf, recording 152 points (42 goals, 110 assists) and 1,254 penalty minutes. Can you name him?
Hint: He was elected to the Hall of Fame.

2) Signed as a free agent on October 25, 1944, this goalie played in 50 games for the Maple Leafs in 1944–45, posting a 24–22–4 record during the regular season. The Calder Trophy–winning rookie netminder took the Leafs to the Stanley Cup in 1945 by recording four shutouts (including three straight during the finals against Detroit). Despite his impressive first season, he played only one more year with the Leafs before his NHL career was over. Name him.

3) This defenceman from Winnipeg, Manitoba, played five games for the Maple Leafs in 1945–46 and became a regular the following season. He was a low-scoring rearguard (he did not score a goal in six seasons) but he was very reliable in his own end and could make good passes from the point on the power play. He was with the Leafs for four Stanley Cups and was named team captain in 1956. Toronto dealt him to Chicago (where he played in 1957–58), but not before he had played in 717 games and recorded 223 points in a Maple Leaf uniform. Who was he?

4) This left winger from Toronto, Ontario, first joined the Maple Leafs in 1946–47 when he got into 14 regular-season games. He won his first Stanley Cup in 1948 and was called up from the minors for the 1949 playoffs, recording a hat trick in game against Detroit to help secure his second championship. He became a Leaf regular in 1949–50, scoring 20 or more goals in six straight seasons and netting 33 in 1954–55.

Toronto's Peter Stemkowski (#12) keeps his eye on NHL All-Star Bobby Orr.

Named captain of the team in 1955, he was a two-time winner of the Lady Byng Trophy and made the NHL's second All-Star team on one occasion. Who was he?

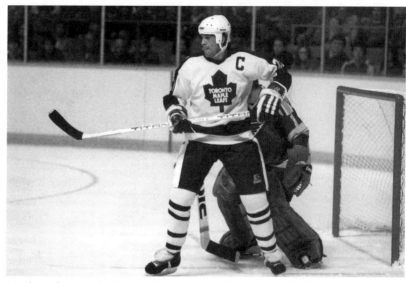
Maple Leaf captain Rick Vaive (#22) was never afraid to stand in front of the net.

5) A native of Calgary, Alberta, this right winger joined the Maple Leafs in 1952–53, scoring 13 goals and totalling 35 points in 70 games. He stayed with Toronto until the end of the 1964–65 season, primarily in a checking role, although he did score 21 times in 1958–59. He won three Stanley Cups with the Leafs in the 1960s, but was traded to Boston in the summer of 1965 for three players: Orland Kurtenbach, Pat Stapleton and Andy Hebenton. He also played for the Rangers, Canucks and Islanders before he tried coaching the New York Rangers and the Los Angeles Kings. Who was he?

6) This netminder from Port Colborne, Ontario, was acquired by the Maple Leafs from Boston for Ed Chadwick on January 31, 1961. The goalie the Leafs received was in net the night the Leafs won the Stanley Cup on April 22, 1962, the first of three Toronto championships he was part of. Who was he?

7) Claimed by the Maple Leafs from Boston in the Intra-League Draft of 1960, this native of Kirkland Lake, Ontario, joined the team for the 1960–61 season and was in and out of the Leaf lineup over the next few seasons. In

1966–67 he was a regular on the Toronto defence and was an important part of the team that won the Stanley Cup (his second championship with the blue and white). Two years later he was in Montreal, where he won another Cup in 1969. Who was he?
Hint: He also played for Detroit, Boston, Minnesota, Philadelphia, Los Angeles and Buffalo.

8) A former rookie of the year (in 1955), this right winger was the captain of the Chicago Blackhawks the last time they won the Stanley Cup in 1961. The Maple Leafs claimed him on waivers from Detroit on December 29, 1961, and he helped Toronto win three straight Cups between 1962 and 1964. His NHL career ended after the 1963–64 season. Who was he?

9) The Maple Leafs sent four players to Springfield of the American Hockey League in June of 1962 for this defenceman who was a native of Cobalt, Ontario. The robust blueliner joined the Leafs for the 1962–63 season and

won the Calder Trophy as the NHL's best rookie (with seven goals and 22 points) at the age of 27. He was with Toronto for three Stanley Cups, but was lost to Oakland in the Expansion Draft of 1967. He later played for Detroit. Who was he?

10) The Maple Leafs signed this free agent in August of 1963, and he spent most of his time

Centre Bill Derlago (#19) came to the Maple Leafs in a trade with Vancouver.

with Toronto in the minors. However, he played in three playoff games in 1967 (his only games as a Leaf) and got his name on the Stanley Cup as a result. He joined Minnesota for 35 games in the 1967–68 season and another

18 contests in 1968–69. In total he recorded 22 points in 54 games for the North Stars before his NHL days were over. Who was he?

11) A graduate of the Toronto Marlboros, the big winger (six foot three, 197 pounds) joined the Maple Leafs on a full-time basis in 1966–67, when he scored 14 goals during the regular season. He was superb in the '67 playoffs, contributing three goals and two assists in 12 games, earning his place on the Stanley Cup–winning team. He scored the game-winner in the fifth game of the finals (a 4–1 win played in Montreal). He spent the 1967–68 season with the Leafs, scoring 11 goals, but was gone from the NHL after one more season with Detroit. Who was he?

12) A highly touted defenceman on the strength of his play in junior hockey with the Toronto Marlboros (he was compared to Bobby Orr at that point), this blueliner played in 594 career games and recorded a very respectable 327 points (81G, 246A) with the Maple Leafs. He had five seasons of 30 or more assists and also played right wing at times. He was in Toronto until the 1977–78 season and finished his career with 10 games as a Minnesota North Star. Who was he?
Hint: This player has been a longtime sportscaster with CITY-TV in Toronto.

13) The Maple Leafs picked up this winger from Oakland in a deal that saw them send Gerry Ehman to the Seals. He played in only one game for the Leafs (recording one assist) during the 1967–68 season before he was dealt to Minnesota in a trade that mostly involved minor-league players. As a North Star he flourished, scoring 20 or more goals three

times and being named to Team Canada in 1972. He also played for the New York Islanders and the Cleveland Barons. Who was he?
Hint: His son made it to the NHL with the New Jersey Devils and scored 31 goals in 2006–07.

Maple Leaf defenceman Jim Thompson (middle of photo) stands in front of goaltender Harry Lumley during this game in Chicago against the Blackhawks.

14) Drafted 55th overall in 1969, this tough left winger joined the Maple Leafs for nine games in 1969–70 and then for 50 games during the 1970–71 season. He scored nine goals (three in one game versus Pittsburgh) in 1970–71 but was claimed in the 1972 Expansion Draft by the New York Islanders. He went on to play for Buffalo and Pittsburgh, recording 223 points in 553 games. Who was he?
Hint: His nickname was "Spinner."

15) Drafted 11th overall by the Maple Leafs in 1972 after a great career with the Toronto Marlboros, this centreman scored 10 goals in his rookie year but would never net more than 19 for the Leafs in any one season. He was traded to Pittsburgh along with Randy Carlyle for Dave Burrows, and he promptly put together four consecutive 20-goal seasons (21, 21, 25 and 22). He finished his career with two years in Minnesota. Name him.

16) Signed as a free agent along with Borje Salming, this Swedish-born left winger scored 20 goals in 1973–74, his first year with the Maple Leafs. He followed that up with seasons of 21, 19 and 24 but was traded away to St. Louis for forward Jerry Butler. Who was he?

17) This speedy left winger set a Maple Leaf team record by scoring a goal in 10 consecutive games during the 1984–85 season, a year that saw him score 30 or more goals for the fourth consecutive time. The Toronto Marlboro graduate was originally drafted by the Leafs (11th overall) in 1977. By the 1978–79 season he had established himself as a consistent goal scorer with 25 markers. The Leafs foolishly traded him in the summer of 1985 to the Quebec Nordiques for Brad Maxwell. Who was he?

18) This big defenceman (six foot four, 210 pounds) was drafted third overall by the Maple Leafs in 1982 and he played in 16 games for Toronto in 1982–83. Serious knee injuries hampered him in his first two seasons, but he got into 76 contests (recording 20 points)

in his third year and then 79 games in 1985–86, a year that saw his play improve greatly. A contract dispute saw him sign with Chicago as a free agent, and the Leafs were compensated for their loss with the likes of Jerome Dupont and Ken Yaremchuk. Who was he?

19) Selected seventh overall by the Maple Leafs in 1983, this speedy centre took his time

Defenceman Larry Hillman was outstanding for the Maple Leafs during the 1967 playoffs.

developing but then put together three consecutive seasons of 20 or more goals. He had 29 goals and 73 points in 1986–87 for Toronto, but just two years later he was traded to Montreal for John Kordic. Name him.

20) Toronto management surprised the hockey world once again when they traded perennial 50-goal scorer Rick Vaive, along with Steve Thomas and Bob McGill, to Chicago for Al Secord (a complete bust as a Maple Leaf) and this centre, who was a native of the Windy City. He scored a career-high 42 goals for Toronto in 1987–88 and then had 90 points the following year. After an 88-point season in 1989–90, he was dealt to Winnipeg in November 1990 for Dave Ellett. Name him. *Hint: He was with the New York Rangers when they won the Stanley Cup in 1994.*

21) A December 17, 1990, deal saw the Maple Leafs send defenceman Brian Curran and Lou Franceschetti to Buffalo for a big right winger who was captain of the Sabres. He scored 13 goals for the Leafs in 1992–93 while playing in just 55 games. However, he is best remembered for scoring an overtime goal during the fifth game of the '93 playoff series against Detroit that gave Toronto a 3–2 lead in games. He finished his career with the Florida Panthers in 1993–94. Who was he?

22) A Hall of Fame right winger, he joined the Maple Leafs in a trade with the New York Rangers in 1994 that saw Toronto send Glenn Anderson to New York. His best moment with Toronto came in the '94 post-season, when he scored an overtime winner against the San Jose Sharks — a goal that kept the Leafs alive in the series. He scored 35 times for the Leafs in 1995–96 but was dealt to Phoenix before the next season. Who was he? *Hint: He scored 708 career goals and also played for Washington and Minnesota.*

23) Signed as a free agent by the Maple Leafs in 2001, this left winger led the team in points with 79 (33 goals, 46 assists) in 2002–03, breaking Mats Sundin's eight-year run as the Leafs' leading point-getter. He also won the Lady Byng Trophy while with Toronto. Can you name him?
Hint: He is the only Leaf player to wear sweater number 89.

Toronto's Brian Conacher (#22) tries to keep the puck away from Larry Jeffrey of the New York Rangers. Both players were on the Leafs' Stanley Cup team of 1967.

24) The Maple Leafs signed this free-agent netminder to back up Curtis Joseph for the 2001–02 season, and he got into 30 games, posting a very respectable 12–10–5 record. However, Toronto could not sign him for the following season and he returned to New Jersey, where he backed up Martin Brodeur. He got his name on the Stanley Cup when the Devils took the trophy in 2003. Who was this netminder?

25) Hoping to add a quality veteran for a late-season push, the Maple Leafs traded two players (Alyn McCauley and Brad Boyes) and a first-round draft choice to the San Jose Sharks for this feisty right winger who would play a total of 79 games (26 goals) with Toronto before leaving the team. He did nothing for the Leafs in the playoffs (missing the 2004 post-season with a knee injury) and signed with Phoenix for the 2006–07 season. Name him.
Hint: He was selected first overall by Quebec in 1990.

26) This large (six foot three, 215 pounds) native of Toronto joined the Maple Leafs as a free agent prior to the 2005–06 season. He was originally drafted by the Washington Capitals in 1993 but had his most productive seasons with Boston and Los Angeles. He had 60 points (17 goals, 43 assists) in 66 games but was deemed too slow for the "new NHL." Who was he?

27) It was a lifelong dream for this centreman to play for the Maple Leafs, and it came true in 2005–06 after he signed as a free agent with Toronto. He had scored 356 goals and logged 827 points in his career to that point, and he scored a goal in his first game as a Leaf on October 4, 2005, against the Ottawa Senators. But injuries limited him to just 33 games, in which he recorded 22 points. He signed with Dallas for the 2006–07 season. Can you name him?

28) Drafted 65th overall by the Maple Leafs in 2001 after a good career with the Ottawa 67's of the

Ed Olczyk (#16) was a player the Maple Leafs were interested in acquiring for a long time, and they finally got him in a trade with Chicago in 1987.

OHL, defenceman Brendan Bell never really got an opportunity to play a steady role with Toronto. He managed one goal and five points in 2006–07, but was traded to Phoenix along with a draft choice for a player who was joining the Leafs — for the third time! Can you name the player the Leafs received from the Coyotes?

DID YOU KNOW?

1) Play-by-play broadcaster Foster Hewitt was the man most responsible for making the Maple Leafs into Canada's team during the "Original Six" era. Prior to the advent of television, Canadians would gather around their radios to listen to the early days of *Hockey Night in Canada*. What was Hewitt's signature phrase to introduce each game?

2) On February 17, 1927, Toronto's NHL entry played its first game ever as the Maple Leafs. They were previously known as the St. Patricks, but new owner Conn Smythe felt the maple leaf was a Canadian symbol recognized across the country (and he had worn maple leaf badges on his army uniform). What was the result of the first game played under the new nickname, and who scored the first Maple Leaf goal?

3) This Maple Leaf played in only one NHL game — on December 13, 1930 — and he scored a goal in Toronto's 7–3 loss to the Boston Bruins. He was the first NHL player to have the distinction of scoring a goal in his only contest. Can you name him?

4) This goaltender set an NHL record by recording a shutout in each of the first five games of the 1930–31 season (beating Ottawa 2–0 on November 22, 1930, to establish the mark) and would become the first Maple Leaf netminder to record 100 wins. Who was he? *Hint: He was the Leafs' goalie when they won the Stanley Cup in 1932.*

5) When the Hockey Hall of Fame officially opened in Toronto on August 26, 1961, on the grounds of the Canadian National Exhibition, among the new members elected were four players who had been with the Maple Leafs in the 1930s and '40s. Name all four.

6) On December 20, 1950, this Maple Leaf became the first goalie in franchise history to

record 300 career victories when Toronto beat Montreal 6–1. Name the netminder.

7) There is only one Maple Leaf coach who had his son play on the team while he was behind the Toronto bench. The son was called up from the junior Toronto Marlboros for three games in total. Who were the coach and player?

8) A February 26, 1966, contest saw the Maple Leafs beat Boston 3–2, and this player became the first to score 250 goals in a Toronto uniform. Who scored the milestone maker?

9) The Maple Leafs had Johnny Bower and Terry Sawchuk as their main goalies for the 1966–67 season, but three other netminders also played for Toronto that season. Veteran Bruce Gamble (who played in 23 games) was one of them, while the other two shared a common surname. Can you name both?

10) Prior to the start of the 1967 playoffs, the Maple Leafs made a major change to their uniform. What was the change?
Hint: It involved the team crest.

11) Perhaps the most important goal the Maple Leafs scored in the 1967 playoffs came in the third game of the Stanley Cup finals, which went into double overtime at the Gardens. The series was tied at one game each, but Toronto needed a home win if they hoped to beat

Montreal. From a face-off in the Canadiens' end of the ice, the Leafs worked the puck around until they found an open man who simply redirected the puck past Rogie Vachon of the Habs. Who scored the goal?

12) On February 28, 1968, this Maple Leaf forward began a streak of 914 consecutive games played when Toronto beat Boston 1–0 at the Gardens. He only played 15 games for the Leafs before he was traded to the Detroit Red Wings. He also played for St. Louis, Atlanta, Los Angeles and Edmonton. Can you name him?

13) He is the only Maple Leaf ever to take penalty shots in consecutive games when he scored against Detroit on March 9, 1968, during a 9–5 Toronto victory, and then was stopped by Denis DeJordy of Chicago the next day, during a 4–0 loss to the Blackhawks. Who was he?
Hint: He was a member of the 1967 Stanley Cup team and went by the nickname "Shakey."

Goaltender Gary "Suitcase" Smith (#1) played five career games for the Maple Leafs.

14) The Maple Leafs got bombed in Boston to the tune of 10–0 on April 2, 1969, during the first game of the playoffs. It was a fight-filled contest, and Boston superstar Bobby Orr was knocked out by a devastating body check (and part elbow) delivered by this Toronto defenceman. Who was the rugged Leaf blueliner that enraged the fans at Boston Garden that night?

15) When the Maple Leafs beat the Blackhawks 6–2 on January 3, 1970, it meant that this Leaf player had appeared in games in each of four decades (1940s, '50s, '60s and '70s). Who was he? *Hint: He was a longtime captain of the Leafs, and holds the team record for most games played.*

16) Three players who were members of the 1971–72 Maple Leafs were selected to play for Team Canada in the Summit Series. Name all three. *Hint: Two were forwards and one was a defenceman.*

17) During the 1970s, NHL goaltenders begain painting their masks. Most designs featured the team logo in some way, and that was true of this Leaf netminder, who put a big, blue maple leaf on his mask. Who was the goalie?

18) The squad assembled for the first-ever Canada Cup tournament in 1976 may have been the best team this country has ever organized. Two members of the 1975–76 Maple Leafs made that edition of Team Canada. Name both. *Hint: Both were forwards.*

19) Despite a 97-point season with the Maple Leafs in 1980–81, this big right winger was dealt away to the Quebec Nordiques for Miroslav Frycer on March 9, 1982. He also

is the only Leaf to wear sweater number 99. Who was he?

20) This player scored four goals in a game against the Maple Leafs on two different occasions (the first on January 22, 1976, versus goalie Gord McRae, and the second on October 27, 1979, against netminder Paul Harrison) while he was a member of the Los Angeles Kings. He coached the Kings briefly and later coached the Maple Leafs for two seasons in the 1990s. Who was he?

21) On May 4, 2002, the Maple Leafs played in the fourth-longest playoff game in their

Paul Henderson scored many big goals for Team Canada in 1972 including the series winner over the Russians.

Eric Lindros was a Maple Leaf for the 2005–06 season.

history when they hosted the Ottawa Senators in the Eastern Conference semi-finals. It wasn't until the third overtime period (and 44:30 of extra time had been played) before this winger scored to give Toronto a 2–1 win. Who scored the goal?

22) After an outstanding career that included Stanley Cup wins with the Calgary Flames, Dallas Stars and New Jersey Devils, this centre signed with the Maple Leafs as a free agent in 2003. He scored 22 goals in the regular season and six more in the 2004 playoffs. He signed with Florida in 2005, but had to retire one year later. Who is he?

23) Drafted 57th overall in 2002, this centre joined the Maple Leafs for his first game on April 5, 2003, and scored a goal against the Ottawa Senators at the Air Canada Centre. Who is this player who scored a goal in his first NHL game?

24) This player is the only Maple Leaf to score the team's lone goal on a penalty shot in a 1–0 Toronto victory. It happened on March 19, 2006, at Pittsburgh, and it was the second time in NHL history that a game winner in a 1–0 game had been scored this way. Which Leaf scored the goal and which Penguin goalie did he beat?

25) The Maple Leafs set a team record when they won their 26th game on home ice, beating Pittsburgh 5–3 on April 18, 2006. One of the Leaf goals in the contest was scored by a Leaf rookie who was playing his first game for the team. Who scored the goal?

26) When the Carolina Hurricanes won the Stanley Cup in 2006, they did so by beating the Edmonton Oilers 3–1 in the seventh game of the finals. The Carolina defenceman who scored the Cup-winning goal has a brother on the Maple Leafs who is also a rearguard. Can you name both of them?

27) During the summer of 2006, Maple Leaf general manager John Ferguson Jr. was determined to bolster the Toronto blueline brigade, so he signed two free-agent defencemen. One was a member of the Tampa Bay Lightning when they won the Stanley Cup in 2004, while the other was a longtime member of the Boston Bruins. Name both.

Goaltender Doug Favell played in 74 games with the Maple Leafs, posting a 26–26–16 record.

28) While playing junior hockey in Belleville, this small centre led the Ontario Hockey League with 118 points (35G, 83A) in 2000–01. He was traded by Belleville to Windsor for Jason Spezza during the 2001–02 season and played minor pro with St. John's of the American Hockey League. He joined the Leafs for the 2005–06 season and recorded 45 points in 81 games. Who is he?

ANSWERS

BOSTON BRUINS

MEMORABLE GAMES

1) The Bruins edged the Montreal Maroons by a 2–1 score.
2) Montreal won the game 1–0.
3) Bill Carson
4) For the first time all year, the Bruins lost two consecutive games, and that allowed Montreal to sweep the best-of-three finals.
5) Roy Conacher
6) Dit Clapper scored his 200th NHL goal in the game versus Toronto.
7) Bobby Bauer
8) The Bruins scored four overtime goals to take the contest 6–2.
9) Milt Schmidt scored his 200th career goal as the Bruins beat Chicago 4–0.
10) Henry recorded three straight shutouts (6–0 over Montreal, 1–0 over New York and 3–0 over Toronto) on home ice. Henry played in all 70 games for the Bruins in 1953–54.
11) Willie O'Ree played for the Bruins in a 3–0 win over the Habs.
12) Don Simmons
13) Jerry Toppazzini
14) Derek Sanderson passed Orr the puck from behind the Blues' net, which was occupied by goaltender Glenn Hall.
15) Ken Dryden
16) Wayne Cashman
17) Bobby Clarke
18) Rick Middleton and Terry O'Reilly
19) Bobby Schmautz

Ray Bourque

Barry Pederson

27) Brian Leetch
28) Alex Ovechkin of the Washington Capitals

RECORDS AND AWARDS

1) Eddie Shore
2) Bill Cowley
3) Milt Schmidt led the NHL in scoring with 52 points in 48 games, while Woody Dumart was second with 43. Bobby Bauer also recorded 43 points, but with five fewer goals than Dumart, he was ranked third. The three all played on the same line, known as the Kraut Line and the Kitchener Kids.
4) Herb Cain
5) Tiny Thompson
6) Frank Brimsek
7) Sam LoPresti

20) Bourque took off his sweater to reveal one with number 77 sewn on it. From that point on, Bourque's new number was 77, and 7 stayed retired.
21) A power failure at the Garden made it impossible for the fourth game of the series to continue, and the game was officially suspended. The Oilers took the Cup on home ice two nights later with a 6–3 win.
22) Petr Klima
23) Ron Tugnutt
24) Sandy Moger scored the opening goal, while Cam Neely got the hat trick.
25) Ray Bourque beat Felix Potvin at 19:22 of the third period to send the Bruins' fans home happy.
26) Joe Thornton

Rick Middleton

Don Marcotte

Wings 5–4. Bucyk scored on Yves Belanger of St. Louis on October 30, 1975, in a 3–2 Boston victory.

15) Jean Ratelle

16) Reggie Lemelin shared the trophy with Moog.

17) Barry Pederson

18) Joe Juneau

19) Phil Esposito (1974), Barry Pederson (1982) and Cam Neely (1988). Neely's big night came on the road during a 10–3 win in Chicago.

20) Ray Bourque

21) b) 4: Phil Esposito (five times), Johnny Bucyk (once), Ken Hodge (once) and Cam Neely (twice).

22) Chris Nilan

23) Jarno Kultanen

24) Bill Guerin in 2002 and Joe Thornton in 2003

25) Patrice Bergeron

26) Zdeno Chara

27) Marc Savard

28) Defenceman Dennis Wideman

8) Jack Gelineau

9) Larry Regan

10) Eddie Johnston

11) Ed Van Impe

12) True. Orr won the Hart (most valuable), Art Ross (most points), Norris (best defenceman) and Conn Smythe (best player in the playoffs) trophies.

13) Johnny Bucyk

14) Esposito scored his goal against Jim Rutherford of Detroit on December 22, 1974, when the Bruins beat the Red

Defenceman Mike Milbury (#26) chases a Buffalo Sabre.

TRADES

1) Marty Barry
2) Herb Cain
3) Johnny Bucyk
4) Dean Prentice
5) Reggie Fleming and Ab McDonald
6) Johnny McKenzie
7) Boston sent Leo Boivin and forward Dean Prentice to Detroit in exchange for Doak, Ron Murphy and Bill Lesuk.
8) The Bruins acquired Esposito, Ken Hodge and Fred Stanfield in exchange for Gilles Marotte, Pit Martin and Jack Norris.
9) Danny Schock and Rick MacLeish
10) The Bruins sent Rick Smith, Reggie Leach and Bob Stewart to the Seals, while the Bruins received Vadnais and Don O'Donoghue.
11) Gilles Gilbert
12) Fred O'Donnell and Chris Oddleifson
13) Ken Hodge
14) Peter McNab
15) Ron Grahame
16) A second-round draft choice (used to select Steve Konroyd in 1980) and a third-round draft choice (used to select Mike Vernon in 1981)
17) Pete Peeters
18) The Kings received a first-round draft choice in 1985 (with which they collected Dan Gratton).
19) The Bruins gave up Barry Pederson in the trade and received a first-round draft choice with which they selected Glen Wesley third overall in 1987.
20) Geoff Courtnall, Bill Ranford and a second-round draft choice in 1988
21) Bobby Carpenter
22) Kyle McLaren (1995), Jonathan Aitken (1996) and Sergei Samsonov (1997)
23) Washington acquired Bill Ranford, Rick Tocchet and Adam Oates from Boston. The Bruins also got goalie Jim Carey as part of the trade.
24) The Sharks sent goaltender Jeff Hackett and defenceman Jeff Jillson to Boston.
25) Sergei Gonchar
26) Brad Stuart, Marco Sturm and Wayne Primeau
27) Defenceman Paul Mara
28) Andrew Ference and Chuck Kobasew

Gord Kluzak

REMEMBER HIM?

1) Cy Denneny
2) Eric and Gord Pettinger
3) Pat Egan
4) Bill Quackenbush
5) Bronco Horvath

Al "Junior" Langlois

6) Leo Labine
7) Real Chevrefils
8) Ed Sandford
9) Charlie Burns
10) Vic Stasiuk
11) Fern Flaman
12) Tommy Williams
13) Gary Dornhoefer
14) Jean-Guy Gendron
15) Ted Green
16) Don Marcotte
17) Jim Lorentz is the player and Ron Plumb was taken ninth overall in 1970 with the draft choice the Bruins received in the deal.
18) Ross Brooks
19) Gregg Sheppard
20) Mike Milbury
21) John Wensink

22) Butch Goring
23) Gord Kluzak
24) Don Sweeney
25) Brian Rolston
26) Dave Scatchard
27) Craig MacTavish
28) Tom Fitzgerald

DID YOU KNOW?

1) Harry Oliver
2) Dit Clapper recorded a hat trick in a game that featured a bench-clearing brawl that forced the Boston police to move in and break it up.
3) Art Ross
4) Thompson became the first goalie to record an assist in an NHL game.
5) There were no penalties called in the entire game!
6) New York Rangers
7) Lynn Patrick
8) Boston won the Saturday night contest in Toronto 11–0, beating former Bruin goaltender Don Simmons for all the goals!
9) Pit Martin
10) The two points earned against Chicago lifted the Bruins past the Rangers, who had 47 points in 1965–66 — marking the first time since 1960 that Boston did not finish in last place.
11) Al "Junior" Langlois
12) Lorne "Gump" Worsley
13) Wayne Rivers
14) Bobby Orr, Dallas Smith, Johnny Bucyk, Phil Esposito, Ken Hodge and Ed Westfall all played in the game for the East Division, while Harry Sinden coached.
15) Johnny Bucyk, Ed Westfall and Ted Green
16) Peter McNab (41 goals), Terry O'Reilly (29), Bobby Schmautz (27), Stan Jonathan (27), Jean Ratelle (25), Rick Middleton (25), Wayne

Cashman (24), Gregg Sheppard (23), Brad Park (22) and Don Marcotte (20)

17) Rick Middleton

18) Ken Linseman was traded to Philadelphia for Dave Poulin.

19) Adam Oates

20) Gordie Roberts

21) The game was played in Atlanta as part of the NHL's series of neutral-site games played that season.

22) Al Iafrate

23) Sergei Samsonov

24) Tuukka Rask

25) Glen Murray

26) Tim Thomas

27) Jordan Sigalet

28) The Detroit Red Wings, for the 2002–03 and 2003–04 seasons. Lewis was fired in June 2007 and replaced by Claude Julien.

Bobby Orr

CHICAGO BLACKHAWKS

MEMORABLE GAMES

1) Pittsburgh Pirates
2) Stewart Adams
3) Johnny Gottselig scored the winner in Chicago and Cy Wentworth scored the winner at the Montreal Forum, but the Canadiens took the Cup 3 games to 2.
4) Harold "Mush" Marsh
5) Alf Moore beat the Leafs 3–1.
6) Carl Voss
7) Virgil Johnson
8) Moe Roberts played the final 20 minutes of the game, allowing no goals, in a 6–2 Chicago win over the Detroit Red Wings.
9) Bill Mosienko scored the hat trick and Gus Bodnar helped out on all three goals.
10) Al Dewsbury
11) Bill Mosienko
12) Bobby Hull
13) Reggie Fleming
14) Murray Balfour
15) Ab McDonald
16) Eric Nesterenko
17) Lorne "Gump" Worsley
18) Montreal took the game 4–0 and regained the Stanley Cup for the first time in five years.
19) Cesare Maniago
20) The victory assured Chicago of first place overall with a 41–17–12 record.
21) Tony Esposito was the goalie, and he beat the Toronto Maple Leafs for his 15th shutout.
22) Bobby Hull
23) Jim Pappin
24) Chris Chelios, Jeremy Roenick and Steve Larmer
25) The Leafs won 1–0, eliminating the Blackhawks from the playoffs.
26) San Jose Sharks
27) Martin Havlat
28) Peter Bondra

Bobby Hull

RECORDS AND AWARDS

1) Cully Dahlstrom
2) Les Cunningham
3) The Bentley brothers, Doug (who won the Art Ross Trophy in 1943) and Max (who won the

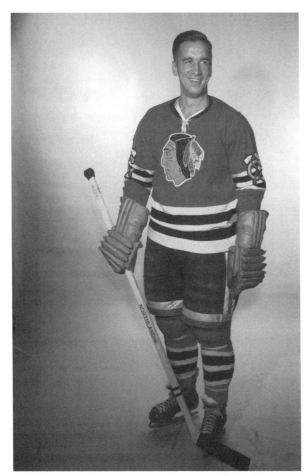

Ted Lindsay

award in 1946 and 1947)

4) Roy Conacher

5) Al Rollins

6) He started the season with the Montreal Canadiens, but was sent to the Blackhawks on December 10, 1954, as part of a league-wide effort to help the Chicago franchise, which was struggling badly at the time.

7) Tommy Ivan

8) Pierre Pilote

9) Goaltender Glenn Hall

10) Stan Mikita

11) Ken Wharram

12) b) 5. Bobby Hull scored 50 or more five times as a Blackhawk.

13) Philadelphia Flyers

14) Pat Stapleton

15) Ed Giacomin of the New York Rangers

16) Billy Reay

17) Cesare Maniago

18) Orval Tessier

19) Behn Wilson

20) Troy Murray (1986) and Dirk Graham (1991)

21) Ed Belfour

22) Pit Martin

23) Denis Savard

24) Steve Larmer

25) Chicago has topped 100 points six times (reaching 107 twice to set the team record) and earned one Presidents' Trophy, in 1990–91 when they notched 106 points.

26) Bryan Berard

27) Adrian Aucoin

28) Brent Seabrook

TRADES

1) Lionel Conacher

2) Leroy Goldsworthy, Lionel Conacher and Roger Jenkins

3) Bill Thoms

4) Jim Henry, who played one season (1948–49) in Chicago before being traded to Detroit

5) Clare Martin, George Gee, Max McNab, Jimmy Peters and Jim McFadden all won the Cup with Detroit. Clare "Rags" Raglan was the other player acquired in the deal.

6) Allan Stanley, Nick Mickowski and Dick Lamoureux

7) Ted Lindsay came to Chicago, while the Blackhawks gave up Forbes Kennedy, Johnny Wilson, Hank Bassen and Bill Preston.

8) Doug Mohns

9) Al Rollins, Gus Mortson and Cal Gardner were the '51 Leafs; Ray Hannigan was also included in the deal.

10) Gerry Desjardins, Bill White and Bryan Campbell

11) Gary Smith came to Chicago in exchange for Kerry Bond, Gerry Pinder and Gerry Desjardins.

12) Dale Tallon came to Chicago in return for Jerry Korab and Gary Smith.

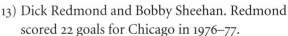
Goaltender Ed Belfour stops Toronto's Peter Zezel.

13) Dick Redmond and Bobby Sheehan. Redmond scored 22 goals for Chicago in 1976–77.

14) Curt Fraser

15) Adam Creighton

16) Steve Smith

17) Eric Daze

18) The Blackhawks acquired Gary Suter (along with Randy Cunneyworth) in exchange for Frantisek Kucera and Jocelyn Lemieux.

19) Chicago added Bryan Marchment to the trade and received Eric Weinrich and Patrick Poulin in return.

20) Alexei Zhamnov and Craig Mills, were the players while Ty Jones was chosen with the draft pick.

21) Chris Terreri, Ulf Dahlen and Michal Sykora

22) Tyler Arnason

23) Tom Preissing and Josh Hennessy

24) Chicago also got Bryan Smolinski, and they sent Tom Preissing, Josh Hennessy and Michal Barinka to Ottawa along with the draft choice.

25) Michael Handzus

26) Radim Vrbata

27) Tony Salmelainen

28) Jason Williams

REMEMBER HIM?

1) Charlie Gardiner

2) Paul Thompson (brother of Cecil "Tiny" Thompson)

3) Earl Seibert

4) Clint Smith

Denis DeJordy

Bill White

5) Lee Fogolin Sr.
6) Jack "Tex" Evans
7) Elmer Vasko
8) Chico Maki
9) Al MacNeil
10) Doug Jarrett
11) Mike Veisor
12) Keith Magnuson
13) Cliff Koroll
14) John Marks
15) Bob Murray
16) Ivan Boldirev
17) Jack O'Callahan
18) Tom Lysiak
19) Murray Bannerman
20) Darryl Sutter
21) Keith Brown

22) Mike Peluso
23) Michel Goulet
24) Stu Grimson
25) Steve Sullivan was dealt for two second-round draft choices, one each in 2004 (Ryan Gerlock) and in 2005 (Michael Blunden).
26) Trent Yawney
27) Matthew Barnaby
28) Eric Daze

DID YOU KNOW?

1) Cully Dahlstrom, Roger Jenkins, Virgil Johnson, Mike Karakas, Alex Levinsky, Doc Romnes, Louis Trudel and Carl Voss
2) Bill Stewart
3) Reg Bentley scored the goal and was set up by his brothers Max and Doug.
4) Doug Bentley, Bud Poile and Gaye Stewart. Bentley had an assist and Stewart scored a goal.

Gary Suter

5) Sid Abel

6) Dick Irvin

7) Red Storey decided he would resign when he did not get the support of his boss.

8) Rudy Pilous

9) Bill Hay and Murray Balfour

10) Wayne Hillman

11) Eric Nesterenko

12) Chicago won all four games, the last coming at the Montreal Forum on October 30, 1965, when the Blackhawks beat the Canadiens 6–4.

13) Lou Angotti

14) Bruce Gamble

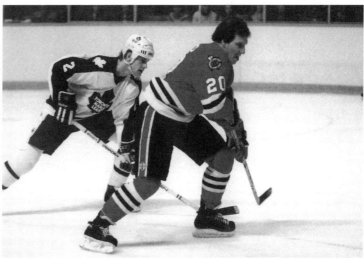

Chicago's Al Secord (#20) tries to break away for a scoring chance.

Doug Wilson

15) Stan Mikita, Eric Nesterenko, Dennis Hull and Ken Wharram

16) Grant Mulvey

17) Bobby Orr

18) Doug Wilson

19) Al Secord (once) and Jeremy Roenick (twice)

20) Denis Savard

21) Darren Pang

22) Chris Chelios

23) Tony Amonte

24) Sergei Krivokrasov

25) Glenn Hall (#1), Bobby Hull (#9), Stan Mikita (#21) and Tony Esposito (#35)

26) Tuomo Ruutu

27) Rene Bourque

28) Patrick Lalime

Gordie Howe

MEMORABLE GAMES

1) Modere "Mud" Bruneteau
2) Johnny Sorrell
3) Pete Kelly
4) Earl Robertson
5) Carl Liscombe
6) Syd Howe
7) Billy Taylor
8) Johnny Mowers
9) Pete Babando
10) Terry Sawchuk
11) Tony Leswick
12) Ted Lindsay
13) Gordie Howe
14) Gerry Melnyk scored the winner, but the Leafs won the series in six games.
15) Charlie Hodge
16) Terry Sawchuk set a new NHL record with his 95th career shutout, surpassing the mark held by George Hainsworth.
17) Larry Jeffrey
18) Norm Ullman
19) Petr Klima
20) All four games in the series were decided by the same 4–2 score.
21) Atlanta Flames
22) Nicklas Lidstrom scored the winner on June 1, Vladimir Konstantinov on June 6 and Vyacheslav Kozlov on June 11 to send Detroit to the Stanley Cup finals against New Jersey.
23) Darren McCarty
24) Kris Draper
25) Igor Larionov
26) Paul Kariya
27) Marcus Nilson and Martin Gelinas
28) Kirk Maltby scored for Detroit and Jarret Stoll scored for Edmonton.

RECORDS AND AWARDS

1) New York Rangers
2) Syd Howe
3) Don Grosso
4) Goaltender Roger Crozier
5) Red Kelly
6) Alex Delvecchio
7) Terry Sawchuk (three times) and Glenn Hall (once)
8) Howie Young

9) Norm Ullman
10) False. Gordie Howe won the award six times, but Ted Lindsay won the Art Ross Trophy in the 1949–50 season.
11) b) 3: Ebbie Goodfellow in 1940, Sid Abel in 1949 and Sergei Fedorov in 1994
12) Les Binkley
13) John Ogrodnick
14) Mickey Redmond scored the goal against Ron Low.
15) Marcel Dionne
16) Brad Park
17) Tom Barrasso of Pittsburgh (1987–88), Eldon "Pokey" Reddick of Winnipeg (1988–89), Glenn Healy of New York Islanders (1989–90), Mike Richter of New York Rangers (1990–91) and Bill Ranford of Edmonton (1992–93).
18) Bob Probert

Bill Gadsby

Terry Sawchuk

19) Chris Osgood, with 32
20) Detroit won 62 games (during the 82-game regular-season schedule), the most ever by one team in a single season.
21) Dino Ciccarelli
22) Five times (1995, 1996, 2002, 2004 and 2006), the most of any team
23) Bobby Kromm (1978), Jacques Demers (twice — 1987 and 1988) and Scotty Bowman (1996)
24) Roger Crozier (1966), Mike Vernon (1997), Steve Yzerman (1998) and Nicklas Lidstrom (2002)
25) b) 6: Gordie Howe, Alex Delvecchio, Steve Yzerman, Dino Ciccarelli, Pat Verbeek and Brendan Shanahan
26) Detroit beat Anaheim on March 1 by a score of 2–0 and beat St. Louis 3–2 on April 15.
27) Pavel Datsyuk
28) Henrik Zetterberg

TRADES

1) Normie Smith
2) Joe Carveth
3) Al Dewsbury, Harry Lumley, Jack Stewart, Pete Babando and Don Morrison went to Chicago in exchange for Goldham, Metro Prystai, Gaye Stewart and Jim Henry.
4) Tony Leswick
5) Bill Gadsby
6) Doug Barkley
7) Roger Crozier and Ron Ingram
8) Detroit picked up defenceman Leo Boivin and forward Dean Prentice in return for Ron Murphy, Gary Doak and Bill Lesuk and future considerations (which turned out to be the rights to Steve Atkinson).
9) Tom Webster

Red Kelly

10) Red Berenson and Tim Ecclestone
11) Goaltender Joe Daley
12) Dan Maloney and Terry Harper
13) Bryan Watson
14) Detroit sent Foligno, Brent Peterson and Dale McCourt to Buffalo for Danny Gare, Jim Schoenfeld and Derek Smith.
15) Murray Craven and Joe Paterson
16) Bernie Federko and Tony McKegney
17) Petr Klima, Adam Graves, Jeff Sharples and Joe Murphy
18) Igor Larionov
19) Detroit sent Carson, along with Marc Potvin and Gary Shuchuk, to Los Angeles in return for Paul Coffey and journeymen Sylvain Couturier and Jim Hiller.
20) Steve Chiasson
21) Dan McGillis

Roger Crozier

Danny Gare

7) Earl Reibel
8) Bill Dineen
9) Marty Pavelich
10) Tommy Ivan
11) Jimmy Skinner
12) Bruce MacGregor
13) Gary Bergman
14) Parker MacDonald
15) Nick Libett
16) Jim Rutherford
17) Reed Larson
18) Gerard Gallant
19) Shawn Burr
20) Viacheslav Fetisov
21) Joe Kocur
22) Martin Lapointe

22) Detroit sent Keith Primeau and Paul Coffey to the Whalers, while Brian Glynn accompanied Shanahan to the Red Wings.
23) Anders Eriksson
24) Vyacheslav Kozlov
25) Kris Draper
26) Mathieu Schneider
27) Robert Lang
28) Todd Bertuzzi

REMEMBER HIM?

1) Larry Aurie
2) Ebbie Goodfellow
3) Herbie Lewis
4) Marty Barry
5) Leo Reise Jr.
6) Jim McFadden

Randy Ladouceur

23) Brett Hull
24) Mathieu Dandenault
25) Manny Legace
26) Curtis Joseph
27) Luc Robitaille
28) Jiri Fischer

DID YOU KNOW?

1) Jack Adams
2) Detroit beat Chicago 3–1 on home ice.
3) Doug Young
4) Eddie Bush
5) Doug McKay
6) Harry Lumley
7) Dave Gatherum
8) b) 6: Howe scored three goals (his 12th career hat trick) and added three assists to total six points in the contest.

Gordie Howe, Alex Delvecchio and Norm Ullman

9) Gordie Howe and Ted Lindsay were the players threatened. Lindsay scored the winning goal.
10) Billy Dea
11) Nick Mickowski, Bob Bailey, Hec Lalonde and Jack McIntyre
12) Howe recorded his 1,000th career point in the NHL.
13) Val Fonteyne
14) Alex Faulkner
15) Danny Grant
16) Henry Boucha
17) Johnny and Larry Wilson
18) Michel Bergeron
19) Vaclav Nedomansky
20) The game ended in a 4–4 tie with Greg Joly of the Red Wings getting the final goal.
21) Randy Ladouceur wore number 19 prior to Yzerman, while Danny Gare captained the club in 1982–83.
22) Dean Morton
23) Dale McCourt in 1977 and Joe Murphy in 1986
24) Bowman won his 1,000th career NHL game.
25) Alex Delvecchio's
26) Tomas Holmstrom
27) Mike Babcock
28) Daniel Cleary

MEMORABLE GAMES

1) Joe Malone

2) Georges Vezina

3) Montreal won the game 14–7 with Newsy Lalonde scoring six times for the Canadiens.

4) Montreal beat Quebec 16–3, setting a record for most goals in one game by one NHL team.

5) Howie Morenz scored the goals against the Calgary Tigers.

6) Billy Boucher scored the first goal after 56 seconds of play, and the Canadiens went on to beat the Toronto St. Patricks.

7) Johnny Gagnon scored the winner, while George Hainsworth got the shutout.

8) Paul Bibeault allowed the goals, while the three stars of the game were Maurice Richard, Maurice Richard and Maurice Richard!

9) Harry Lumley

10) Maurice Richard scored what was his most dramatic goal against Jim Henry of the Bruins.

11) Jacques Plante

12) Elmer Lach scored the winner while Gerry McNeil earned the shutout.

13) Bernie Geoffrion

14) Jean Beliveau scored the goals and was assisted on all three by Bert Olmstead.

15) Andy Bathgate

16) Bobby Rousseau scored five goals on Roger Crozier of the Red Wings.

17) Claude Provost

18) Jean Beliveau scored the goal and was named the first-ever winner of the Conn Smythe Trophy. Gump Worsley was the netminder who gained a rather easy shutout.

19) Henri Richard

20) Jacques Lemaire made it 2–1 on a blast from 65

Yvan Cournoyer

feet out and Henri Richard tied the game 2–2.

21) Yvan Cournoyer

22) Steve Shutt, Yvon Lambert and Yvan Cournoyer

23) Guy Lafleur

24) Eric Desjardins scored the winner and had all the Montreal goals that night, making him one of the few defencemen in the history of the NHL to record a hat trick in a playoff game.

25) Montreal beat the Dallas Stars 4–1, and Andrei Kovalenko scored the last goal at the Forum.

26) Sidney Crosby

27) Jan Bulis

28) Michael Ryder scored for Montreal on April 24, while Eric Staal and Cory Stillman won the games played on April 26 and May 2, 2006, respectively.

RECORDS AND AWARDS

1) Gus Rivers

2) Maurice Richard

3) Maurice Richard

4) Maurice Richard beat Glenn Hall of Chicago for his 500th goal.

5) The Habs took the Cup in eight straight games by sweeping Chicago and Toronto, just as Detroit had done in '52 when they took out Toronto and Montreal with 4–0 series wins.

6) a) George Hainsworth. He recorded 75 career shutouts for the Habs, while Plante had 58, Dryden is next with 46 and Durnan had 34.

7) Bill Durnan (1944–47, 1949 and 1950) and Jacques Plante (1956–60 and 1962)

8) Bernie Geoffrion (1952) and Ralph Backstrom (1959)

9) Bobby Rousseau (1962) and Jacques Laperriere (1964)

Guy Lafleur

10) Montreal players have won the Conn Smythe Trophy nine times: Jean Beliveau (1966), Serge Savard (1969), Ken Dryden (1971), Yvan Cournoyer (1973), Guy Lafleur (1977), Larry Robinson (1978), Bob Gainey (1979) and Patrick Roy (twice, in 1986 and 1993).

11) Maurice Richard, 1956; Dickie Moore, 1957; Bernie Geoffrion, 1958; Marcel Bonin, 1959; and Jean Beliveau, 1960

12) Charlie Hodge won the award in 1963–64 and shared it with Gump Worsley in 1965–66.

13) John Ferguson

14) Frank Mahovlich

15) Peter Mahovlich finished the 1974–75 season with 117 points.

16) The Canadiens recorded 132 points in 1976–77 based on a record of 60–8–12 during the 80-game regular schedule and then took the Stanley Cup for the second year in a row.

17) Guy Lafleur was given the Lester B. Pearson Trophy in 1976, 1977 and 1978.

18) Jean Beliveau, Frank Mahovlich, Henri Richard and Guy Lafleur

19) Jacques Lemaire in 1977 and 1979, and Mario Tremblay in 1978

20) Doug Harvey (six times), Tom Johnson (once), Jacques Laperriere (once) and Larry Robinson (twice)

21) Brian Skrudland

22) Lyle Odelein

23) Jacques Plante (in 1962) and Jose Theodore (in 2002)

24) Doug Jarvis

25) Bob Gainey won the Frank J. Selke Trophy four times (1979 through to 1981) and was the Habs' general manager in 2006–07 while Guy Carbonneau won the Selke three times (1988, 1989 and 1992) and was the Canadiens coach in 2006–07.

26) Steve Begin

27) Serge Savard (#18) and Ken Dryden (#29)
28) Patrick Roy (who also won with Colorado) and Dick Duff (the Leafs)

TRADES

1) Aurel Joliat
2) The Habs acquired Hector "Toe" Blake in return for Lorne Chabot.
3) Albert "Babe" Siebert
4) Billy Reay
5) Buddy O'Connor
6) Ab McDonald
7) Gump Worsley, Leon Rochefort, Dave Balon and Len Ronson
8) Ken Dryden
9) Ted Harris

Rick Wamsley

Ralph Backstrom

10) The Canadiens selected goalie Michel "Bunny" Larocque.
11) Danny Grant and Claude Larose
12) Claude Larose, who would help Montreal win the Stanley Cup in 1971 and 1973.
13) Mickey Redmond, Bill Collins and Guy Charron
14) Montreal selected Mario Tremblay 12th overall.
15) Robert Picard
16) Rick Green and Ryan Walter
17) Mark Napier, Keith Acton and a second-round draft choice (with which Minnesota selected Ken Hodge Jr.)
18) Goaltender Patrick Roy was selected 57th overall in 1984.

Pierre Larouche

REMEMBER HIM?

1) Sprague Cleghorn
2) Pit Lepine
3) Sylvio Mantha
4) John Quilty
5) Emile "Butch" Bouchard
6) Andre Pronovost
7) Bob Turner
8) Dollard St. Laurent
9) Al "Junior" Langlois
10) Gordon "Red" Berenson
11) Lou Fontinato
12) Al MacNeil
13) Gilles Tremblay
14) Terry Harper
15) Jimmy Roberts
16) Pierre Larouche
17) Cam Connor
18) Pat Hughes
19) Steve Penney

19) Shayne Corson was selected 8th overall in the first round and Stephane Richer was taken 29th in the second round of the draft.
20) Sylvain Turgeon
21) Tom Chorske and Stephane Richer
22) Vincent Damphousse
23) Jocelyn Thibault, Andrei Kovalenko and Martin Rucinsky
24) Sheldon Souray
25) David Aebischer
26) Niklas Sundstrom
27) Cristobal Huet
28) Mike Johnson

Jean-Guy Talbot

20) Kjell Dahlin
21) Gilbert Dionne
22) Mats Naslund
23) Brian Bellows
24) John LeClair
25) Pierre Turgeon
26) Ron Hainsey
27) Defenceman Janne Niinimaa
28) Craig Rivet was traded by Montreal to San Jose for Josh Gorges.

Larry Robinson

Steve Shutt

DID YOU KNOW?

1) b) Maurice Richard. The words are taken from Roch Carrier's classic children's story *The Hockey Sweater.*
2) Jean-Guy Talbot
3) J. C. Tremblay
4) The goalies were Charlie Hodge and Garry Bauman. Henri Richard was named as the MVP of the game with a goal and an assist.
5) Rogie Vachon
6) Rejean Houle and Marc Tardif. Houle was also on the Stanley Cup teams of 1977, 1978 and 1979.
7) Yvan Cournoyer, Ken Dryden, Guy Lapointe, Frank Mahovlich, Peter Mahovlich and Serge Savard
8) Tony Esposito
9) Claude Ruel

10) Steve Shutt

11) Once. Lafleur scored four on January 26, 1975, when Montreal beat Pittsburgh 7–2.

12) Patrick Roy

13) Larry Robinson

14) d) The Canadiens record for their first 5,000 games was 2,625 wins, 1,603 losses and 722 ties.

15) Scotty Bowman (1977) and Pat Burns (1989)

16) False. The 1973–74 Canadiens recorded 99 points (45–24–9 in 78 games). All of Bowman's other teams in Montreal had over 100 points.

17) Toe Blake was named as coach; Jacques Plante in goal; Doug Harvey and Larry Robinson on defence; and Jean Beliveau (centre), Maurice Richard (right wing) and Dickie Moore (left wing) as the forwards.

18) Patrick Roy and Kirk Muller. Roy played the first period, stopping all 11 shots he faced.

19) Guy Carbonneau (two), Kirk Muller (two), Gilbert Dionne, Vincent Damphousse and Stephane Lebeau. The goalie was Patrick Roy.

20) a) Jacques Plante

21) Michael Ryder

22) Alex Kovalev

23) Denis Savard

24) Gino Odjick

25) Saku Koivu

26) Mark Streit

27) Chris Higgins

28) Sergei Samsonov. Samsonov was dealt to Chicago in June of 2007.

Jose Theodore

NEW YORK RANGERS

MEMORABLE GAMES

1) The Rangers beat the Montreal Maroons 1–0 at Madison Square Garden.
2) The Rangers' coach and general manager, 44-year-old Lester Patrick, took over in goal and the New York club was sufficiently inspired to win the game 2–1 in overtime.
3) Frank Boucher
4) The Boston Bruins beat New York for the Cup, and it marked the first time two U.S.–based teams met for the championship.
5) Fred Cook
6) New York beat a very tired (they had played a very long overtime game the previous night) Leaf team 5–1 to open the finals.
7) Bill Cook
8) Walter "Babe" Pratt
9) Dave Kerr
10) Earl Robertson
11) Lorne Carr
12) Mel "Sudden Death" Hill
13) Bryan Hextall
14) Don "Bones" Raleigh
15) Peter Stemkowski
16) Vic Hadfield scored against Denis DeJordy of Montreal.
17) Chicago Blackhawks
18) Rod Gilbert
19) Jean-Paul Parise
20) Phil Esposito
21) Ken Morrow scored against Glen Hanlon of the Rangers.
22) Brian MacLellan scored the first OT winner, and Bob Brooke got the second.
23) Mark Messier on both counts. He issued the guarantee, then backed it up with the three-goal outburst.

Adam Graves

24) Stephane Matteau
25) Brian Leetch, Adam Graves and Mark Messier got the three Ranger goals. Messier's tally in the second period turned out to be the game- and Cup-winner.
26) Roberto Luongo
27) Marek Malik
28) Brendan Shanahan

RECORDS AND AWARDS

1) The Rangers beat the Quakers 3–0.
2) Murray Murdoch
3) Ab DeMarco

Brad Park

4) Chuck Rayner
5) Camille Henry
6) Andy Bathgate
7) Lou Fontinato
8) Andy Hebenton
9) Harry Howell
10) Pierre Jarry
11) Jean Ratelle
12) Rod Gilbert
13) Brad Park
14) Don Murdoch
15) Mikko Leinonen
16) Mark Pavelich
17) John Vanbiesbrouck
18) b) 3. Doug Harvey won it in 1962, Harry Howell in 1967 and Brian Leetch in 1992 and 1997.
19) a) 2. The Rangers had the best record in the NHL in 1991–92 and 1993–94.

20) Adam Graves beat Bill Ranford of Edmonton for the goal.
21) Mike Gartner scored his 500th on Mike Liut of the Washington Capitals on October 14, 1991, while Mark Messier scored his 500th against Rick Tabaracci of the Calgary Flames on November 6, 1995.
22) Mike Gartner (trade with Minnesota), Steve Larmer (trade with Hartford), Pat LaFontaine (trade with Buffalo) and Theoren Fleury (signed as a free agent)
23) Sergei Zubov
24) Brian Leetch
25) Jaromir Jagr
26) Henrik Lundqvist
27) Michal Roszival
28) Jaromir Jagr

Ed Giacomin

TRADES

1) John Ross Roach
2) Butch Keeling
3) Cecil Dillon
4) Art Coulter
5) Allan Stanley
6) Johnny Bower
7) Danny Lewicki
8) Red Sullivan
9) Bill Hicke
10) Ed Giacomin
11) Red Berenson
12) Dave Balon
13) Glen Sather
14) Pete Stemkowski
15) Nick Beverley
16) Gilles Villemure
17) Phil Esposito, Carol Vadnais and Joe Zanuzzi came to the Rangers.
18) Barry Beck
19) Marcel Dionne
20) Tomas Sandstrom and Tony Granato
21) Bernie Nicholls, Louie DeBrusk and Steven Rice
22) Roman Oksiuta and a third-round draft choice in 1993
23) Petr Nedved, Chris Tamer and Sean Pronger
24) Anson Carter
25) Maxim Kondratiev, Jarkko Immonen, a first-round draft choice in 2004 and a second-round pick in 2005
26) Defenceman Paul Mara
27) Marcel Hossa
28) Sean Avery

Earl Ingarfield

REMEMBER HIM?

1) Ivan "Ching" Johnson
2) Ott Heller
3) Mac and Neil Colville. Neil was the one elected to the Hall of Fame.
4) Phil Watson
5) Edgar Laprade
6) Pentti Lund
7) Earl Ingarfield
8) Dean Prentice
9) Walt Tkaczuk
10) Jim Neilson
11) Bill Fairbairn
12) Steve Vickers
13) John Davidson
14) Nick Fotiu
15) Ron Greschner
16) Dave and Don Maloney
17) Ron Duguay
18) Anders Hedberg

19) Ulf Nilsson
20) Mike Rogers
21) James Patrick
22) Kelly Kisio
23) Mike Richter
24) Jeff Beukeboom
25) Esa Tikkanen
26) Herb Brooks
27) Martin Rucinsky
28) Martin Straka

DID YOU KNOW?

1) Rickard was an admirer of the Texas Rangers, the famous law-enforcement agency from that state.

Edgar Laprade and Chuck Rayner

Ron Duguay

2) The Rangers posted a record of 25 wins, 11 losses and 2 ties in Christmas Day games.
3) Frank Boucher
4) John Ross Roach (13 shutouts in 1928–29) and Lorne Chabot (11 in 1927–28 and 10 in 1926–27)
5) Bert Connelly
6) Harry Lumley
7) Muzz's brother Lynn was coaching the Bruins. Muzz, who had recently taken over as Rangers bench boss, won the contest 8–3.
8) Vic Howe, Gordie's brother, who played in a total of 33 NHL games, scored for New York.
9) The New York Rangers!
10) Dave Dryden
11) Andy Bathgate
12) Ulf Sterner
13) Bernie Geoffrion
14) Rod Gilbert
15) The Soviet club won the game 7–3.
16) The members of the line were Jean Ratelle,

Esa Tikkanen

Rod Gilbert and Vic Hadfield, while the moniker stood for "goal a game."

17) Pierre Larouche
18) Guy Lafleur
19) Stephane Matteau and Brian Noonan
20) Craig MacTavish
21) Frank Boucher in 1940 and Mike Keenan in 1994
22) Gretzky recorded one assist, on a goal by Brian Leetch.
23) Kim Johnsson, Jan Hlavac, Pavel Brendl and a third-round draft choice in 2003
24) Pavel Bure
25) Petr Prucha
26) The entire Ranger team would gather at centre ice and raise their sticks to salute the fans.
27) Matt Cullen
28) Michael Nylander

TORONTO MAPLE LEAFS

MEMORABLE GAMES

1) Chicago won the opening game 2–1, and they took the final contest by a score of 6–2. Harold "Mush" Marsh scored the first-ever goal in Toronto's new building in 1931, while Bob Probert scored the final goal in the 68-year-old hockey shrine in 1999.
2) The Leafs beat Chicago and the Montreal Maroons (both in total-goals series) and then knocked off the New York Rangers in three straight games to clinch the championship. Ace Bailey scored the winning goal on Gardens ice.
3) Ken Doraty
4) Dave "Sweeney" Schriner
5) Walter "Babe" Pratt
6) Ted Kennedy
7) Syl Apps, who retired after the 1947–48 season
8) Cal Gardner
9) Tod Sloan
10) Brian Cullen and Sid Smith each scored three times, while Gump Worsley gave up all the goals for the Rangers.
11) Dick Duff scored the game-winning goal, and Montreal beat New York 4–2 giving the Leafs a playoff spot by one point.
12) Dave Keon scored both goals, with the second going into an empty Detroit net.
13) Billy Harris
14) Dave Keon, Red Kelly and George Armstrong
15) Imlach sent out Tim Horton, Red Kelly, George Armstrong, Bob Pulford and Allan Stanley to protect the net occupied by Terry Sawchuk. Stanley took the draw (against Jean Beliveau) and Armstrong scored the goal to make it a 3–1 final score.
16) Jim Harrison
17) Borje Salming
18) Gerry Cheevers, who shut out the Detroit Red Wings 7–0 the next night in Boston
19) Darryl Sittler, with three of his goals coming in the second period
20) Ian Turnbull
21) Doug Gilmour (who had four points on the night) tied the game, while Nikolai Borschevsky won it when he tipped in a shot by Bob Rouse.
22) Wendel Clark scored three goals against Kings netminder Kelly Hrudey. Glenn Anderson was the Leaf who took the penalty. Wayne Gretzky scored the OT winner, but he should have

Darryl Sittler

Mats Sundin

1) Charlie Conacher
2) Harvey "Busher" Jackson
3) Right winger Don Metz
4) Walter "Babe" Pratt (in 1944) and Ted Kennedy (in 1955)
5) Howie Meeker
6) Brit Selby
7) Dick Duff
8) Terry Sawchuk and Johnny Bower. Sawchuk played in 36 of the Leafs' 70 games, while Bower appeared in 34.
9) The shutout was the 100th of Terry Sawchuk's career (he would finish his career with 103).
10) Detroit Red Wings
11) c) 5: George Armstrong, Tim Horton, Borje Salming, Dave Keon and Ron Ellis
12) Ian Turnbull
13) Dave "Tiger" Williams
14) Buffalo's Memorial Auditorium

been penalized for a high stick that cut Leaf forward Doug Gilmour seconds earlier. Referee Kerry Fraser failed to make the call.

23) Kirk McLean
24) Sergei Berezin
25) Miikka Kiprusoff of Calgary allowed the goals, the last of which (scored when the Leafs were short-handed), was an overtime game-winner and the 500th of Sundin's career.
26) Eric Lindros scored for the Leafs against Andrew Raycroft.
27) Jose Theodore
28) The Leafs had the members of the 1967 Stanley Cup team introduced prior to the game (which included the return of Hall of Famer Dave Keon), and the Leafs beat the Edmonton Oilers.

Gary Leeman

15) Toronto beat the Edmonton Oilers, and Miroslav Frycer scored four times for the Maple Leafs.

16) Doug Gilmour

17) Darryl Sittler. He had seven points (three goals, four assists) against the New York Islanders on October 14, 1978, in a 10–7 Toronto victory at Maple Leaf Gardens.

18) The centres were Ted Kennedy, Dave Keon, Doug Gilmour and Mats Sundin; the right winger was Charlie Conacher; and the defenceman was Babe Pratt.

19) Rick Vaive (three times), Gary Leeman (once) and Dave Andreychuk (twice, although part of one year was played with Buffalo)

20) Darryl Sittler and Doug Gilmour. Sittler hit the mark first, when he had an even 100 in

Ron Ellis

1975–76. He also recorded 117 points in 1977–78. Gilmour set the team record in 1992–93, when he had 127 points. He followed up with 111 in 1993–94.

21) Gary Suter of the Calgary Flames

22) Norm Ullman, Glenn Anderson, Doug Gilmour, Larry Murphy, Mats Sundin and Alex Mogilny

23) Pat Burns won the award in 1993, while Pat Quinn was the runner-up in 1999, when Jacques Martin of Ottawa was named the winner. Both achieved their status in their first year with Toronto.

24) Punch Imlach won 365 games (1958–69 and 1979–80), while Pat Quinn won an even 300 (between 1998 and 2006).

Coach George "Punch" Imlach

Darcy Tucker

7) Red Kelly
8) Andy Bathgate and Don McKenney
9) Marcel Pronovost, Larry Jeffrey, Autry Erickson (all three of whom were on the '67 Cup team), Lowell MacDonald and Ed Joyal
10) Frank Mahovlich, Peter Stemkowski, Garry Unger and the rights to Carl Brewer
11) Jim Pappin
12) Bernie Parent was the goalie, and Rick Kehoe was selected by the Leafs with the draft pick.
13) Tim Horton
14) Toronto selected Ian Turnbull with the pick and later received netminder Eddie Johnston.

25) Dave Keon and Ron Ellis
26) Wade Belak
27) Borje Salming (#21), Red Kelly (#4) and the late Hap Day (also #4)
28) Andrew Raycroft

TRADES

1) Francis "King" Clancy
2) Harvey Jackson, Buzz Boll, Murray Armstrong and Doc Romnes
3) Frank Eddolls
4) Max Bentley and Cy Thomas
5) Allan Stanley
6) Eddie Shack

Ron Stewart

Foster Hewitt

25) Mike Johnson and Marek Posmyk
26) Alexei Ponikarovsky
27) Alexander Suglobov
28) Tyson Nash

REMEMBER HIM?

1) Red Horner
2) Frank "Ulcers" McCool
3) Jim Thomson
4) Sid Smith
5) Ron Stewart
6) Don Simmons
7) Larry Hillman
8) Eddie Litzenberger

15) Toronto selected Bob Neely, and Doug Favell was the goalie sent to the Leafs to complete the deal.
16) Paul Gardner
17) Wilf Paiement and Pat Hickey
18) Rick Vaive and Bill Derlago
19) Darryl Sittler
20) Bob Rouse and Peter Zezel
21) Grant Fuhr, Glenn Anderson and Craig Berube
22) Gary Leeman, Michel Petit, Alexander Godynyuk, Craig Berube and Jeff Reese
23) Mats Sundin, Garth Butcher, prospect Todd Warriner and Quebec's first-round pick
24) Jason Smith, Steve Sullivan and Alyn McCauley

Frank Mahovlich

Gary Roberts

9) Kent Douglas
10) Milan Marcetta
11) Brian Conacher
12) Jim McKenny
13) J. P. Parise, father of Zach
14) Brian Spencer
15) George Ferguson
16) Inge Hammarstrom
17) John Anderson
18) Gary Nylund
19) Russ Courtnall
20) Ed Olczyk
21) Mike Foligno
22) Mike Gartner
23) Alex Mogilny

24) Corey Schwab
25) Owen Nolan
26) Jason Allison
27) Eric Lindros
28) Yanic Perreault

DID YOU KNOW?

1) "Hello Canada, and hockey fans in the United States and Newfoundland."
2) The Maple Leafs beat the New York Americans 4–1 at home, with George "Paddy" Patterson scoring the first goal.
3) Rolly Huard
4) Lorne Chabot
5) Charlie Conacher, Hap Day, George Hainsworth and Syl Apps
6) Turk Broda
7) Punch Imlach called up son Brent for two games in the 1965–66 season and for one game on December 25, 1966 (Brent's final NHL appearance).
8) Frank Mahovlich
9) Gary Smith and Al Smith (no relation)
10) In celebration of the country's centennial, the maple leaf emblem was changed from a 35-point leaf to a stylized, 11-point version that matched the one on Canada's flag.
11) Bob Pulford
12) Garry Unger
13) Mike Walton
14) Pat Quinn
15) George Armstrong
16) Paul Henderson, Ron Ellis and Brian Glennie
17) Doug Favell
18) Darryl Sittler (who scored the tournament clinching goal for Canada) and Lanny McDonald
19) Wilf Paiement
20) Mike Murphy

21) Gary Roberts

22) Joe Nieuwendyk

23) Matt Stajan

24) Chad Kilger scored against Marc-Andre Fleury of Pittsburgh.

25) Jeremy Williams

26) Frantisek Kaberle scored the goal for Carolina. His brother, Tomas, plays for the Leafs.

27) Pavel Kubina and Hal Gill

28) Kyle Wellwood

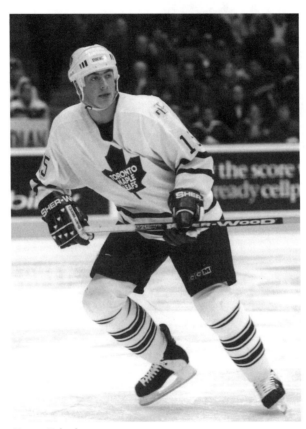

Tomas Kaberle

Acknowledgements

The author would like to thank the following writers for their works on hockey:

Kerry Banks, Dan Diamond (ed.), Dick Irvin, Liam Maguire, Brian McFarlane, Andrew Podnieks, Don Weekes, Ron Wight and Eric Zweig.

Sources consulted: *Hockey News*, *The NHL Guide and Record Book* and the *Stanley Cup Playoffs Fact Guide* (various issues of each) and *Total Hockey*.

Various issues of the Media and Fact Guides for each of the following teams: Boston Bruins, Chicago Blackhawks, Detroit Red Wings, Montreal Canadiens, New York Rangers and Toronto Maple Leafs.

The author would like to say a special thank you to Paul Patskou for his invaluable research on many of the questions that appear in this book.

A special thanks to Maria and David Leonetti for their support and understanding.

Photo Credits

All photographs from the **Harold Barkley Archive** except the following:

Dennis Miles: 9(top), 14(top), 32, 38, 40, 45, 49, 54, 55, 57, 58, 60, 61, 62, 66, 67, 71(bottom), 79(top), 80, 81, 82, 83, 84, 85, 86, 87, 93, 95, 98, 106, 110, 112, 115, 116, 125, 127, 130, 131, 132, 135, 136, 140, 143, 144, 145, 146(bottom), 147(top), 153(top), 154, 155, 161, 162, 164(top), 165, 166, 167, 168(top), 171, 173, 175(top), 177, 178

National Archives of Canada: 75(e002343742)

Robert B. Shaver: 17, 43, 44, 65, 109, 114, 146(top), 147(bottom), 148, 159, 163(top), 170(bottom)

Toronto Star/**Boris Spremo:** 142

York University: 90 (0-303), 91 (0-304), 94 (0-296)